Reflections on the Dark Side of Human Nature

C. P. Kumar
Reiki Healer & Author
Roorkee - 247667, India

Disclaimer

While every effort has been made to ensure the accuracy and completeness of the content in this book, the author cannot guarantee that the information contained herein is error-free, up-to-date, or suitable for every individual circumstance.

The author shall not be held liable or responsible for any errors or omissions in the content of the book, nor for any damages, or losses that may arise from any actions taken based upon the suggestions or contents presented in the book.

Readers are advised to use their own judgment and discretion in applying the information provided in this book, and to consult with qualified professionals before taking any action based on the contents of this book. The author disclaims any and all liability or responsibility for any actions taken or not taken based on the information contained in this book.

DEDICATION

To those brave enough to confront the shadows within,

This book is dedicated to the seekers of truth, the explorers of the human psyche, and the champions of self-awareness. In embarking on this journey through "Reflections on the Dark Side of Human Nature", we acknowledge the courage it takes to face the complexities of our existence and delve into the recesses of our shared humanity.

To those who understand that within each of us lies a duality - a delicate dance between light and darkness - we extend our gratitude for your willingness to reflect on the profound intricacies that shape our thoughts, actions, and interactions.

As we unfold the chapters, each dedicated to illuminating a different facet of the shadows that linger within us, we honor those who approach these reflections with an open heart and a curious mind. This dedication is a testament to your commitment to understanding, not judging, the negative aspects of our human nature.

May this exploration into the roots of violence, cruelty, coercion, corruption, and other challenging aspects of our existence serve as a guide for introspection and a catalyst for positive change. To those who embark on this contemplative journey, we invite you to reflect on the shadows within, recognizing that it is through understanding that we can strive for a brighter, more compassionate world.

With profound appreciation for your courage and curiosity,

C. P. Kumar

CONTENTS

PREFACE

In the vast tapestry of human existence, we are often drawn to the luminous threads of virtue and nobility that define our collective narrative. However, woven intricately amidst the brilliance lies a complex and often disquieting tapestry of shadows - reflections of the darker facets of our nature that silently shape the contours of our lives. It is to this enigmatic terrain that "Reflections on the Dark Side of Human Nature" extends an invitation, beckoning readers into a contemplative exploration of the profound complexities that exist within us all.

The journey begins with a prologue, setting the stage for a reflective odyssey into the depths of human nature. Acknowledging the dualities inherent in our existence, we delve into the shadows that linger, exploring both the light and the darkness that coexist within individuals and society. The intention is not to cast judgment but to seek understanding - a nuanced exploration of negative human attributes and behaviors.

As we embark on this introspective voyage, the subsequent chapters unfold like chapters in the book of humanity. Each one unfurls a new layer, a thematic progression that navigates the intricate corridors of our darker inclinations.

From the roots of violence and environmental exploitation to the complexities of sexual violence and the misuse of power, each chapter addresses a facet of the human experience that resides in the shadows. We explore the web of lies, the consequences of greed, the various faces of discrimination, and the perils of overestimating self-worth. With a critical lens, we scrutinize white-collar crimes, the impact of theft, and the consequences of apathy. The digital age brings forth cyber shadows, while the harsh reality of street harassment and the complexities of addiction paint additional strokes on this multifaceted canvas.

As our journey nears its conclusion, the final chapter invites readers to reflect on the shadows within themselves and society. Summarizing key themes, exploring potential solutions, and encouraging introspection, this concluding chapter aims to leave readers not with despair, but with a sense of empowerment to navigate the complexities of our shared humanity.

In "Reflections on the Dark Side of Human Nature", we traverse the intricate landscape of our shadows, inviting readers to confront the uncomfortable, challenge preconceptions, and ultimately, foster a deeper understanding of the rich, complex mosaic that is the human experience.

C. P. Kumar
Reiki Healer & Author
Former Scientist 'G', National Institute of Hydrology
Roorkee - 247667, India
Web: https://www.angelfire.com/nh/cpkumar/virgo.html

In the vast expanse of human existence, a profound journey awaits - one that leads us into the intricate folds of our own nature. "Reflections on the Dark Side of Human Nature" is not merely a book but an invitation to explore the shadows that linger within us. This endeavor is a contemplative voyage into the complexities of human character, a journey that delves into the duality inherent in our being, acknowledging both the radiant light that illuminates our virtues and the profound darkness that shrouds our vices.

Reflecting on Duality

As we embark on this introspective journey, we find ourselves confronted with the constant interplay between light and shadow. The dichotomy of good and evil, kindness and cruelty, altruism and selfishness - we are, each of us, a living paradox. This exploration is not an exercise in passing moral judgment but a reflective endeavor into understanding the dual nature that resides within individuals and permeates society as a whole. It is an acknowledgment that the shades of gray in our character are as real and integral as the vibrant colors of our virtues.

Seeking Understanding, Not Judgment

The intention here is not to condemn but to foster a deeper comprehension of the shadows that shape our actions. By delving into the nuances of negative human attributes and behaviors, we hope to uncover the roots and motivations that drive us toward darkness. In understanding, there lies the potential for growth and transformation. The shadows are not to be feared but embraced, for it is only through acknowledgment that we can strive for the light.

An Invitation to Contemplation

Dear reader, consider this an invitation to join us on a contemplative exploration. Open your mind to the darker corners of our nature, acknowledging the discomfort that may arise. As we navigate through the shadows, we encourage you to reflect on the impact these hidden facets have on our lives, relationships, and the world around us. It is in this introspective journey that we find the key to unlocking a deeper understanding of ourselves and the human condition.

Thematic Progression: Unveiling the Shadows

In the chapters that follow, we will embark on a thematic progression through the shadows that haunt our collective existence. Each chapter will focus on a specific aspect of negative human behavior, unraveling the complexities and consequences associated with it. This journey is not a detached observation but an immersive exploration into the recesses of our shared humanity.

As we progress through the subsequent sections, we will continue to peel back the layers of darkness, examining corruption, dishonesty, greed, discrimination, and various other shadows that cast a pall over the human experience. The intent is not only to expose these shadows but to foster a collective understanding that paves the way for positive change.

"Reflections on the Dark Side of Human Nature" invites you to confront the shadows within, to question, reflect, and ultimately, to emerge from the journey with a heightened awareness of the intricate tapestry of our shared humanity. Join us as we navigate the labyrinth of the human psyche, seeking not only to understand the shadows but to transcend them. This is not a voyage for the faint of heart but for those brave enough to confront the complexities of their own existence and contribute to a collective understanding that transcends judgment.

Introduction

The human experience is a tapestry woven with threads of light and darkness, good and evil. Within the complex folds of our psyche, the propensity for violence lurks, a shadow that has accompanied humanity throughout its history. To truly understand the roots of violence, one must delve into the intricate web of psychological factors that contribute to aggressive behavior. In this exploration, we unravel the layers that conceal the origins of violence and shed light on the darker recesses of human nature.

Evolutionary Legacy

At the dawn of humanity, survival was the ultimate imperative. The evolutionary legacy imprinted on our species is a primal instinct for self-preservation. Violence, in its rawest form, was a tool for securing resources, defending territory, and establishing dominance. Millennia later, remnants of this ancestral legacy persist within the human psyche, manifesting as aggression in response to perceived threats. Understanding the roots of violence requires acknowledging the deep-seated survival mechanisms that continue to influence human behavior.

Neurobiology of Aggression

Within the intricate circuitry of the human brain, the roots of violence extend into the neurobiological realm. The amygdala, often referred to as the brain's emotional center, plays a pivotal role in processing threats and triggering the fight-or-flight response. When this response is activated, it can lead to aggressive behavior as a means of self-defense.

Furthermore, neurotransmitters like serotonin and dopamine, intricately linked to mood and impulse control, exert a profound influence on the regulation of aggressive tendencies. Examining the interplay of these neurochemical factors provides valuable insights into the physiological roots of violence.

Environmental Influences

While evolutionary and neurobiological factors set the stage, the environment in which an individual is nurtured plays a crucial role in shaping behavioral tendencies. Childhood experiences, exposure to violence, and socio-economic factors contribute to the development of aggressive behavior patterns. The roots of violence often take hold in environments rife with conflict, abuse, or neglect. Understanding the impact of these environmental influences is essential for unraveling the complex tapestry of human aggression.

Socialization and Cultural Norms

Human beings are social creatures, and the roots of violence intertwine with the fabric of societal structures and cultural norms. From a young age, individuals are socialized into a collective understanding of acceptable behavior. In societies where aggression is glorified or normalized, the propensity for violence may be heightened. Examining the role of cultural narratives and societal expectations in shaping human behavior provides valuable insights into the roots of violence on a collective level.

Psychological Trauma

The scars left by psychological trauma can cast a long shadow on an individual's mental landscape, often manifesting in aggressive behavior. Childhood trauma, whether physical, emotional, or sexual, can alter neural pathways and influence the development of maladaptive coping mechanisms. Unraveling the roots of violence necessitates a nuanced exploration of the psychological wounds that fester beneath the surface, sometimes leading individuals down a path of aggression as a means of self-preservation or retribution.

Power Dynamics and Hierarchies

The intricate dance of power within human societies often becomes a breeding ground for violence. As individuals vie for dominance or struggle against perceived oppression, aggression can become a means of asserting control. The roots of violence in power dynamics are deeply embedded in the human psyche, reflecting a struggle for status, resources, or influence. Understanding the psychological underpinnings of power-related aggression is crucial for addressing and mitigating violence on both individual and societal levels.

Group Dynamics and Tribalism

Human history is marked by a tapestry of conflicts fueled by tribalism and group identity. The roots of violence often extend from a primal need to protect one's tribe and vanquish perceived threats from competing groups. In the modern world, this tribalistic mentality can manifest in various forms, from sports rivalries to nationalistic fervor. An exploration of group dynamics and the psychological mechanisms that drive collective aggression unveils the intricate ways in which the dark side of human nature is woven into the social fabric.

Conclusion

In the labyrinth of human nature, the roots of violence extend deep into our evolutionary past, neurobiological makeup, environmental influences, cultural norms, psychological trauma, power dynamics, and group affiliations. Understanding the complexity of these factors is essential for developing strategies to address and mitigate the darker aspects of human behavior. As we reflect on the dark side of human nature, we must strive to illuminate the path towards a more compassionate and harmonious coexistence, where the shadows of violence are gradually replaced by the light of understanding and empathy.

Introduction

The Earth, our home, has been witness to the intricate dance of life for millions of years. However, the dark side of human nature has manifested itself through environmental exploitation. In this exploration, we delve into the profound impact of human actions on the environment and ecosystems, examining the consequences of our collective choices on the delicate balance of nature.

Unveiling the Anthropocene Epoch

The term "Anthropocene" has emerged to define a new geological epoch characterized by the overwhelming influence of human activities on the Earth's geology and ecosystems. As we reflect on the dark side of human nature, it becomes evident that our exploitation of natural resources, deforestation, and pollution have ushered in an era where human actions shape the very fabric of the planet.

The Tragedy of Overconsumption

At the heart of environmental exploitation lies the insatiable human appetite for consumption. The relentless pursuit of economic growth and material wealth has led to the overexploitation of natural resources, pushing ecosystems to the brink of collapse. From deforestation to overfishing, our voracious consumption patterns are driving species to extinction and depleting the Earth's capacity to regenerate.

The Shadow of Industrialization

Industrialization, while transforming societies and economies, has cast a long shadow over the environment. The burning of fossil fuels, release of pollutants, and unchecked industrial activities contribute to air and water pollution, compromising the health of ecosystems. The dark side of industrialization is revealed in the form of smog-filled skies, contaminated rivers, and the ominous threat of climate change.

Plastic Menace

The proliferation of single-use plastics epitomizes the environmental cost of convenience. Discarded plastic waste litters land and sea, posing a grave threat to wildlife and ecosystems. Microplastics infiltrate even the remotest corners of the planet, entering food chains and jeopardizing the health of both terrestrial and aquatic life. *Microplastics are tiny plastic particles, often less than 5 millimeters in size, resulting from the breakdown of larger plastic items or intentionally manufactured at small scales, posing environmental concerns due to their widespread presence and potential ecological impact.* Our synthetic legacy is an enduring testament to the dark side of convenience and consumerism.

Disrupted Ecosystems

Environmental exploitation sets off a domino effect, disrupting interconnected ecosystems. Deforestation not only robs wildlife of their habitats but also destabilizes climate patterns. Pollution in one region can have far-reaching consequences, affecting ecosystems thousands of miles away. The intricate web of life on Earth is unraveling as human actions send shockwaves through the delicate balance of nature.

Extinction Crisis

The dark side of human nature is most vividly illustrated in the current extinction crisis. Rampant habitat destruction, overhunting, and climate change have pushed numerous species to the brink of extinction. The loss of biodiversity not only diminishes the beauty of our planet but also weakens the resilience of ecosystems, making them more susceptible to disease and environmental fluctuations.

Exploitation of Indigenous Wisdom

In the pursuit of progress, we often disregard the wisdom of indigenous communities that have coexisted with nature for generations. The dark side of this neglect is evident in the destruction of traditional knowledge and sustainable practices. The exploitation of natural resources without considering the perspectives of indigenous people further exacerbates environmental degradation, perpetuating a cycle of exploitation.

Ecological Injustice

Environmental exploitation is not a uniform experience for all. Vulnerable communities, often marginalized and disadvantaged, bear the brunt of ecological injustice. From toxic waste dumping in impoverished neighborhoods to the disproportionate impact of climate change on developing countries, the dark side of human nature is starkly evident in the uneven distribution of environmental burdens.

Awakening Consciousness

Despite the grim realities of environmental exploitation, there is a glimmer of hope in the form of an awakening global consciousness. Grassroots movements, environmental activism, and the recognition of the intrinsic value of nature are paving the way for change. Individuals, communities, and nations are increasingly acknowledging the need for sustainable practices and responsible stewardship of the Earth.

Toward a Sustainable Future

As we reflect on the dark side of human nature, it becomes imperative to chart a course toward a sustainable future. Embracing renewable energy, implementing conservation measures, and redefining our relationship with nature are essential steps in mitigating the impact of environmental exploitation. The path to redemption lies in collective action, responsible consumption, and a profound respect for the interconnectedness of all life on Earth.

Conclusion

Beyond cruelty, beyond the shadows cast by the darker facets of human nature, lies the potential for redemption. By acknowledging the consequences of environmental exploitation and taking decisive action, we can steer the course towards a more harmonious coexistence with the planet. The journey toward a sustainable future requires a fundamental shift in our values, behaviors, and the recognition that our fate is intertwined with the well-being of the Earth. In the reflection on the dark side of human nature, we find the motivation to shape a future where environmental exploitation is replaced by a deep and enduring commitment to the preservation of our planet.

Introduction

The pursuit of scientific knowledge has often come at a significant cost, and one of the most contentious aspects of this quest is the use of animals in research. While animal testing has contributed to numerous medical breakthroughs, the ethical concerns surrounding it have sparked debates and raised questions about the moral implications of sacrificing the lives and well-being of innocent creatures. In this article, we will delve into the silent victims of scientific progress - the animals subjected to testing - and explore the dark side of human nature that allows such practices to persist.

The History of Animal Testing

To understand the present ethical concerns surrounding animal testing, it is essential to examine its historical roots. Animal experimentation has a long and complex history, dating back to ancient times. Early scientists, lacking ethical guidelines, conducted experiments on animals with little regard for their welfare. As scientific methods evolved, so did the scale and sophistication of animal testing, leading to the establishment of guidelines and regulations to ensure humane treatment.

The Role of Animal Testing in Scientific Advancements

Proponents of animal testing argue that it has played a crucial role in advancing medical and scientific knowledge. Many breakthroughs, from the development of vaccines to the understanding of diseases, owe their success to experiments conducted on animals. The ability to study physiological and biological processes in living organisms has provided invaluable insights into human health and has saved countless lives.

Ethical Concerns and the Question of Necessity

Despite its contributions to scientific progress, animal testing raises significant ethical concerns. The fundamental question revolves around the necessity of sacrificing animal lives for the betterment of human lives. Critics argue that advancements in technology and alternative methods, such as in vitro testing and computer modeling, have diminished the necessity of using animals in research. *In vitro testing* refers to experiments or studies conducted outside of a living organism, typically in a controlled laboratory setting, to assess biological phenomena, drug efficacy, toxicity, or other biological processes using isolated cells, tissues, or organs. The ethical dilemma lies in determining whether the potential benefits to humans justify the suffering inflicted on animals.

Animal Welfare and the Three Rs

In response to ethical concerns, the scientific community has adopted the "Three Rs" principle - Replacement, Reduction, and Refinement. Replacement involves finding alternative methods that do not use animals. Reduction aims to minimize the number of animals used in experiments, while Refinement focuses on improving the welfare and treatment of animals during testing. Despite these principles, some question the adequacy of their implementation and enforcement.

The Psychological Toll on Animals

Animals used in experiments experience physical and psychological suffering. The confinement, exposure to potentially harmful substances, and invasive procedures inflict pain and distress on these sentient beings. The psychological toll on animals raises questions about the ethical treatment of creatures capable of experiencing fear, anxiety, and pain. Understanding the emotional impact on animals is crucial for addressing the ethical concerns surrounding their use in research.

Speciesism and Moral Considerations

Speciesism is the discrimination or bias in favor of one's own species and against individuals of other species, often manifested in the belief that the interests and rights of one's own species are more important than those of other species. This concept is commonly discussed in the context of ethical considerations related to the treatment of animals and the moral status assigned to different species.

The ethical debate surrounding animal testing is inherently tied to the concept of speciesism - the discrimination against non-human animals based on their species. Critics argue that considering only human interests in scientific research perpetuates speciesist attitudes. Addressing this issue requires a broader ethical framework that takes into account the moral considerations of all living beings, regardless of their species.

Alternatives to Animal Testing

Advancements in technology have paved the way for alternatives to traditional animal testing methods. In vitro testing, computer simulations, and human cell-based models offer promising alternatives that could reduce or eliminate the need for animal experimentation. However, the adoption of these alternatives faces challenges, including scientific validation, regulatory acceptance, and cultural resistance within the scientific community.

Regulatory Oversight and Accountability

Effective regulation and oversight are critical in mitigating the ethical concerns associated with animal testing. Governments and international organizations must establish and enforce stringent guidelines to ensure the ethical treatment of animals in research. Transparency, accountability, and public awareness play pivotal roles in holding institutions and researchers responsible for their actions.

The Road Ahead

As we navigate the complex terrain of scientific progress, it is imperative to strike a balance between advancing human knowledge and respecting the lives and welfare of animals. The ongoing ethical debate surrounding animal testing prompts us to reconsider our priorities and explore innovative methods that align with our moral obligations. The road ahead requires a collective commitment to ethical research practices, the pursuit of alternative methods, and the fostering of a compassionate and inclusive scientific community.

Conclusion

The silent victims of animal testing demand our attention, compassion, and ethical scrutiny. In the pursuit of scientific knowledge, it is essential to reflect on the dark side of human nature that perpetuates practices causing harm to innocent beings. As we grapple with the ethical concerns surrounding animal testing, we must aspire to evolve towards a future where scientific progress coexists harmoniously with a deep sense of responsibility and respect for all living creatures.

Chapter 5. Coercion and Consent
Unraveling the Complexities of Sexual Violence

Introduction

The dark side of human nature encompasses a spectrum of behaviors that delve into the depths of moral, ethical, and societal boundaries. Among these, sexual violence stands out as a profoundly disturbing and complex issue that demands our attention and analysis. In this exploration of the dynamics and impact of non-consensual sexual acts, we delve into the intricate interplay between coercion and consent.

Understanding Consent

Consent is the cornerstone of any healthy sexual encounter. It is a mutual agreement between all parties involved, based on clear communication, willingness, and understanding. Consent is not merely the absence of a "no"; it is an enthusiastic and informed "yes". To truly grasp the complexities of sexual violence, we must first comprehend the essence of consent and how it can be manipulated or violated.

1. The Power Dynamics of Coercion

Sexual violence often stems from power imbalances, where one party exploits their position to coerce another into unwanted acts. This could be in the form of physical force, verbal intimidation, or leveraging authority. In many cases, perpetrators use psychological tactics to undermine the victim's autonomy, creating an environment where resistance feels futile.

The power dynamics at play in coercion are multifaceted, intertwining societal, cultural, and individual factors. Societal norms that perpetuate gender inequality can amplify power differentials, making it easier for some individuals to wield control over others. By examining these dynamics, we can better comprehend the roots of coercion in sexual violence.

2. Manipulation and Gaslighting

Beyond physical force, manipulation and gaslighting are powerful tools used by perpetrators to erode a victim's sense of self and agency. Gaslighting involves the abuser denying or distorting reality, making the victim question their own perceptions. In cases of sexual violence, this manipulation may manifest as the perpetrator convincing the victim that the act was consensual or that they are to blame for the violation.

Unraveling the intricacies of manipulation and gaslighting in the context of sexual violence requires a nuanced exploration of psychological coercion. Understanding how perpetrators exploit vulnerabilities and manipulate emotions sheds light on the insidious nature of non-consensual acts.

Impact on Survivors

1. Physical and Emotional Trauma

The aftermath of sexual violence leaves survivors grappling with profound physical and emotional trauma. The violation of one's autonomy and bodily integrity can result in lasting physical injuries, sexually transmitted infections, and unwanted pregnancies. Moreover, the emotional scars may include anxiety, depression, post-traumatic stress disorder (PTSD), and a profound sense of betrayal.

Exploring the impact of sexual violence on survivors requires acknowledging the depth of trauma inflicted and understanding the long-term consequences that reverberate through various aspects of their lives.

2. Societal Stigma and Victim-Blaming

Another layer of complexity lies in the societal response to survivors of sexual violence. Stigma and victim-blaming often compound the trauma, as survivors may be reluctant to come forward due to fear of judgment or disbelief. Addressing the societal attitudes that perpetuate victim-blaming is crucial in creating an environment where survivors feel supported and empowered to speak out.

Legal and Ethical Considerations

1. Challenges in Legal Frameworks

Navigating the legal landscape surrounding sexual violence poses its own set of challenges. Issues such as the burden of proof, statutes of limitations, and cultural biases within legal systems can hinder justice for survivors. Analyzing the shortcomings in legal frameworks sheds light on the systemic barriers survivors face in seeking accountability for perpetrators.

2. Ethical Responsibility in Prevention

Preventing sexual violence requires a collective commitment to dismantling the societal structures that perpetuate coercion and non-consensual acts. Ethical considerations play a pivotal role in shaping educational programs, fostering consent culture, and dismantling harmful attitudes that contribute to the prevalence of sexual violence.

Conclusion

Coercion and consent exist on opposite ends of a spectrum that defines the boundaries of human interaction. Unraveling the complexities of sexual violence requires a multidimensional approach that examines power dynamics, psychological manipulation, and the profound impact on survivors. By delving into these intricacies, we can work towards fostering a society that not only condemns sexual violence but actively strives to prevent it through education, advocacy, and a commitment to dismantling the dark facets of human nature.

Introduction

Corruption, a pervasive and insidious force, has long haunted societies across the globe. As we delve into the dark recesses of human nature, we confront a phenomenon that transcends borders, cultures, and historical periods. This article aims to explore the multifaceted nature of corruption, unraveling its presence at various levels of society and shedding light on the profound consequences it leaves in its wake.

Defining Corruption

At its core, corruption involves the misuse of power for personal gain, often at the expense of the common good. It manifests in a myriad of forms, from petty bribery to grand-scale embezzlement, infiltrating the very fabric of institutions that are meant to uphold justice and equality. Understanding corruption requires a nuanced examination of its dynamics across different strata of society.

Petty Corruption

In the microcosm of daily life, petty corruption weaves itself into the routine transactions that shape our interactions. Whether it be a traffic stop or a bureaucratic procedure, the demand for bribes can become a normalized part of navigating societal structures. This form of corruption erodes trust in public services, perpetuates inequality, and reinforces a culture of entitlement among those in positions of authority.

Institutional Corruption

Corruption often finds a more entrenched and systemic form within institutions entrusted with safeguarding the public interest. The misuse of power within these structures undermines the very foundations of democracy, justice, and governance. Politically motivated corruption, cronyism, and nepotism can compromise the integrity of entire systems, eroding public trust and fostering a climate of cynicism. *Cronyism* involves favoring individuals based on personal friendships or close relationships, especially in business or politics, rather than on merit or qualifications. *Nepotism* is the practice of showing favoritism toward family members, often in matters of employment or economic opportunities, irrespective of their abilities or qualifications.

Corporate Corruption

The corporate realm is not immune to the allure of corruption. Unethical business practices, bribery, and embezzlement can tarnish the reputation of companies, leading to a loss of investor confidence and public trust. As profit motives overshadow ethical considerations, the consequences of corporate corruption extend beyond financial realms, impacting employees, consumers, and the broader society.

Corruption in Law Enforcement

When corruption infiltrates law enforcement agencies, the consequences are particularly severe. The very entities tasked with upholding justice and maintaining order become complicit in criminal activities. Police corruption, including bribery, extortion, and abuse of power, not only undermines the rule of law but also jeopardizes the safety and well-being of the communities they are meant to protect.

Political Corruption

At the pinnacle of societal hierarchy, political corruption poses an existential threat to democratic principles. When politicians prioritize personal gain over public welfare, the foundations of a just and equitable society begin to crumble. Vote-buying, embezzlement of public funds, and the abuse of political influence erode the democratic process, perpetuating a cycle of corruption that hampers societal progress.

Consequences of Corruption

1. Erosion of Trust

One of the most insidious consequences of corruption is the erosion of trust within society. As citizens lose faith in institutions and their representatives, the social contract that binds communities together weakens. The resulting cynicism can breed apathy, disengagement, and a sense of helplessness among the populace.

2. Inequality and Poverty

Corruption exacerbates existing social inequalities, diverting resources away from essential services and programs meant to uplift the marginalized. The siphoning of public funds for personal gain widens the gap between the privileged few and the disenfranchised many, perpetuating a cycle of poverty and social injustice.

3. Undermining Rule of Law

Corruption weakens the foundations of the rule of law, as legal systems become compromised by bribery, influence peddling, and political interference. When those responsible for upholding justice are themselves implicated in corrupt practices, the legitimacy of legal institutions is eroded, leaving citizens vulnerable to exploitation.

4. Economic Impacts

The economic repercussions of corruption are profound. Foreign direct investment may decline, as investors become wary of the risks associated with corrupt practices. Moreover, the diversion of public funds for personal gain hampers economic development, hindering the potential for sustainable growth and prosperity.

5. Social Unrest

In societies plagued by widespread corruption, a sense of injustice and frustration can fester, leading to social unrest. When citizens perceive that the system is rigged against them, protests and movements may emerge, demanding accountability and systemic change. The consequences of corruption are not confined to the realm of economics and governance; they have the potential to spark widespread social upheaval.

Combating Corruption

1. Strengthening Institutions

Building robust institutions that are transparent, accountable, and free from undue political influence is crucial in the fight against corruption. Implementing and reinforcing mechanisms for oversight, checks and balances, and whistleblower protection can help fortify institutions against the corrosive effects of corruption.

2. Fostering Transparency and Accountability

Promoting transparency is a powerful antidote to corruption. Open access to information, financial transparency, and accountability mechanisms can act as deterrents to corrupt practices. Public awareness campaigns and education about the detrimental effects of corruption play a vital role in fostering a culture that rejects such behavior.

3. Empowering Civil Society

Civil society, including non-governmental organizations, the media, and grassroots movements, plays a pivotal role in holding those in power accountable. Empowering civil society to act as watchdogs and advocates for change can contribute to the exposure and elimination of corruption at various levels.

4. International Cooperation

Given the global nature of many corrupt activities, international cooperation is essential in addressing corruption effectively. Collaboration between countries, sharing information, and harmonizing legal frameworks can help combat transnational corruption and money laundering.

Conclusion

As we reflect on the dark side of human nature, corruption emerges as a pervasive and destructive force that undermines the very foundations of society. From petty bribery in daily transactions to grand-scale political corruption, the consequences of this misuse of power are profound and far-reaching. The fight against corruption requires a multi-pronged approach, encompassing institutional reforms, transparency initiatives, and the empowerment of civil society. Only through concerted efforts at local, national, and international levels can we hope to unmask and dismantle the pervasive influence of corruption, allowing for a brighter and more just future for all.

Chapter 7. The Art of Deception
Unpacking the Layers of Dishonesty

Introduction

In the complex tapestry of human nature, the darker threads of deception and dishonesty are woven seamlessly. To delve into the intricate web of lies, manipulation, and deceit is to explore the often-unsettling reality that exists beneath the surface of our interactions. This article aims to unpack the layers of dishonesty, shedding light on the psychological mechanisms behind lying and manipulation. As we navigate the labyrinth of human deceit, we uncover the nuances of the art of deception that have been both a survival mechanism and a source of moral dilemma throughout history.

The Evolutionary Roots of Deception

Deception, as a facet of human behavior, finds its roots deep within the annals of evolutionary history. Survival of the fittest has driven organisms, including humans, to adapt and develop strategies to outwit competitors and predators. The ability to deceive became a valuable tool in securing resources, forming alliances, and ensuring the propagation of one's genes. As our ancestors evolved, so too did the art of deception, engraining it into the very fabric of our social and cognitive architecture.

The Adaptive Nature of Deceit

Deception, often perceived as a negative trait, serves a dual purpose in human interaction. While it can be employed for nefarious purposes, it also acts as an adaptive mechanism for navigating the complexities of social structures. White lies, omissions, and strategic manipulations can grease the wheels of social cohesion, smoothing interactions and preventing unnecessary conflict. Understanding the fine line between deceit as a survival strategy and deception as a tool of exploitation is crucial in unraveling the layers of dishonesty.

The Psychology of Lying

To comprehend the art of deception, one must delve into the intricate workings of the human psyche. Lying is a complex cognitive process that involves not only the formulation of false information but also the management of emotions, facial expressions, and body language. The reasons behind lying are as diverse as the methods employed. Fear of consequences, desire for personal gain, protection of self-image, and the preservation of relationships all contribute to the intricate tapestry of deception.

The Role of Cognitive Dissonance

Cognitive dissonance, the discomfort arising from holding conflicting beliefs or attitudes, plays a pivotal role in the psychology of lying. Individuals often resort to deception to reconcile contradictory aspects of their lives, smoothing over inconsistencies to maintain a sense of internal harmony. Understanding how cognitive dissonance drives deceptive behavior offers insight into the internal struggles that individuals grapple with when confronted with the truth.

The Social Dynamics of Deception

Beyond individual psychology, the art of deception is deeply intertwined with social dynamics. Societal norms, expectations, and pressures create fertile ground for the cultivation of dishonesty. The fear of judgment, rejection, or isolation can lead individuals to construct elaborate facades, presenting a carefully curated version of themselves to the world. In this social theater, deception becomes not just a personal choice but a survival strategy in the complex dance of human relationships.

Manipulation as a Form of Deception

Manipulation, a close cousin of deception, involves influencing others to act in a way that serves one's interests. This artful practice taps into the vulnerabilities of human psychology, exploiting cognitive biases and emotional triggers. From subtle persuasion to blatant coercion, manipulation takes on various forms, leaving individuals on the receiving end often unaware of the strings being pulled. Unraveling the layers of manipulation reveals the intricate interplay between power, control, and the human propensity for deceit.

The Thin Line Between Deception and Self-Preservation

While deception can be wielded as a weapon for personal gain, it also serves as a means of self-preservation. The gray area between lies that harm and lies that protect blurs the ethical boundaries of dishonesty. Understanding the motivations behind deceptive acts is essential in discerning whether they stem from malicious intent or a genuine desire for self-preservation. This nuanced perspective sheds light on the complex interplay of morality and survival instincts within the human psyche.

The Cost of Deception

The art of deception, though serving evolutionary and social purposes, exacts a toll on individuals and societies. Trust, the bedrock of human relationships, crumbles in the face of deceit. The erosion of trust can have far-reaching consequences, permeating interpersonal connections, institutions, and entire communities. Examining the cost of deception prompts us to question the ethical implications of dishonesty and its potential to undermine the very foundations of human interaction.

Cultivating Honesty in the Face of Deception

In the intricate dance between truth and deceit, cultivating honesty emerges as a moral imperative. Understanding the psychological underpinnings of lying provides a foundation for fostering a culture of transparency and integrity. Acknowledging the vulnerability inherent in honesty and embracing the discomfort of truth-telling can reshape the dynamics of relationships and society at large. The journey towards authenticity requires a collective commitment to dismantling the intricate layers of deception that have woven themselves into the fabric of human nature.

Conclusion

The art of deception, with its evolutionary roots and psychological intricacies, unveils a complex portrait of human nature. As we navigate the layers of dishonesty, we encounter the dual nature of deception as both a survival mechanism and a potential source of harm. Understanding the psychology behind lying and manipulation enables us to unravel the intricacies of human behavior, prompting a reflection on the ethical implications of dishonesty. In the quest for self-awareness and societal harmony, the cultivation of honesty emerges as a beacon guiding us through the labyrinth of deception, encouraging a reevaluation of our relationships, values, and the very essence of our shared humanity.

Introduction

In the grand tapestry of human nature, one thread that often stands out is the dark hue of greed. The insatiable desire for more, at the cost of ethical considerations and communal well-being, has woven a complex narrative throughout history. This article delves into the intricate web of consequences that society faces when confronted with unchecked avarice and self-centeredness. From economic disparities to moral erosion, the repercussions of unbridled greed are far-reaching and demand profound reflection.

The Erosion of Ethics

At the heart of the issue lies the erosion of ethical values. Greed often operates as a corrosive force, eating away at the moral fabric that binds a community together. When individuals prioritize personal gain over collective welfare, the very foundations of trust and cooperation begin to crumble. In the pursuit of wealth, people may engage in dishonest practices, fraud, or exploitation, perpetuating a cycle of moral decay that affects not only individuals but the entire societal structure.

Economic Disparities

Unchecked greed plays a pivotal role in exacerbating economic disparities. As a select few accumulate immense wealth, the majority find themselves relegated to the margins of poverty. The growing divide between the haves and have-nots becomes a breeding ground for social unrest and discontent. This economic inequality not only hampers individual opportunities but also stifles the potential for collective progress, as resources are hoarded rather than distributed for the greater good.

The Illusion of Endless Consumption

Greed often perpetuates the illusion of endless consumption. In a world driven by materialism, the relentless pursuit of wealth fuels a culture of overconsumption. Resources are depleted at an alarming rate, and the environment bears the brunt of this insatiable appetite for more. The ecological consequences, from deforestation to pollution, serve as stark reminders of the toll that unchecked greed takes on the planet. The pursuit of fortune, when divorced from environmental responsibility, becomes a dangerous force that threatens the very sustenance of our world.

Social Fragmentation

The fabric of society is intricately woven with threads of social bonds and communal ties. However, when greed takes center stage, these bonds are often torn asunder. Individuals driven by self-interest may disregard the well-being of their fellow community members, leading to social fragmentation. The erosion of empathy and compassion gives rise to a society where solidarity takes a backseat to personal gain. The consequences are not only felt on an individual level but reverberate through the community, leaving behind fractured relationships and a weakened social fabric.

Impact on Mental Health

The toll of greed extends beyond the externalities of societal structures; it deeply impacts individual mental health. The constant pursuit of wealth and success, driven by avarice, can lead to stress, anxiety, and even depression. The relentless pressure to outdo others and amass more can create a toxic environment where mental well-being becomes a casualty. The emphasis on material success over holistic fulfillment contributes to a society where individuals are left grappling with the emptiness that often accompanies the unquenchable thirst for wealth.

Corruption as a Byproduct

Greed often finds an ally in corruption. When self-interest takes precedence over the common good, individuals in positions of power may succumb to corrupt practices. Bribery, embezzlement, and other forms of corruption become the norm rather than the exception. The rot of corruption, fueled by greed, seeps into the very institutions designed to safeguard societal interests, eroding trust in governance and exacerbating the challenges faced by the most vulnerable members of society.

Short-Term Gains, Long-Term Losses

The pursuit of immediate gains, without consideration for long-term consequences, is a hallmark of unchecked greed. Whether in business practices or policy decisions, the myopic focus on short-term benefits can lead to devastating long-term losses. The financial crises that dot history are often rooted in avarice, where individuals and institutions prioritize immediate profits over sustainable growth. The fallout from such crises is felt across generations, highlighting the enduring impact of prioritizing greed over prudence.

The Antidote: Cultivating a Culture of Empathy

To counter the dark side of human nature manifested through greed, a shift in cultural values is imperative. Cultivating a culture of empathy, where individuals prioritize the well-being of the community over personal gain, can act as a potent antidote. This involves fostering a sense of responsibility and interconnectedness that transcends individual pursuits. Educational institutions, media, and societal norms all play a role in shaping this cultural shift, emphasizing the importance of ethical considerations and collective welfare.

Conclusion

In the intricate dance between light and shadow within the human psyche, the specter of greed casts a long shadow. The societal consequences of unchecked avarice and self-centeredness are profound, affecting economic structures, ethical foundations, and the very fabric of human relationships. As we reflect on the dark side of human nature, it becomes clear that the pursuit of fortune at any cost exacts a toll that extends far beyond individual lives. The challenge lies in recognizing the insidious nature of greed and collectively working towards a more equitable and compassionate world where the pursuit of prosperity is tempered by a sense of responsibility to the greater whole.

Introduction

Human history bears witness to a persistent and troubling aspect of our nature – the tendency to harbor bias and discrimination. In the tapestry of society, the threads of prejudice are woven deep, creating a fabric stained with the ugly face of bias. In this exploration, we delve into the various forms of discrimination that plague humanity across societal lines, examining how these biases manifest and the profound impact they have on individuals and communities.

Racism

Racism stands as one of the most pervasive forms of discrimination, rooted in historical injustices and perpetuated by systemic structures. The insidious nature of racism transcends borders, affecting individuals based on the color of their skin. From colonialism to the present day, the deep-seated biases against certain racial groups have led to disparities in education, employment, and opportunities, creating an enduring legacy that stains the pages of history.

Sexism

Gender-based discrimination, or sexism, remains a formidable force that permeates societies worldwide. Women, historically marginalized, continue to face unequal treatment in various spheres of life. From wage gaps in the workplace to gender-based violence, the battle of the sexes rages on, fueled by deeply ingrained stereotypes and societal expectations. Unraveling the layers of sexism exposes the harsh reality that many women confront on a daily basis.

Homophobia and Transphobia

Homophobia refers to negative attitudes, beliefs, or discriminatory behaviors directed towards individuals who are homosexual or perceived to be so. It can manifest as prejudice, bias, or hostility against individuals with same-sex attractions. *Transphobia* involves prejudice, bias, or discrimination against transgender or gender non-conforming individuals. It includes negative attitudes, stereotypes, and discriminatory actions based on a person's gender identity or expression.

Prejudice against individuals based on their sexual orientation or gender identity takes shape in the form of homophobia and transphobia. The LGBTQ+ community grapples with discrimination, ranging from social exclusion to legal hurdles. As societies evolve, there is a growing awareness of the need for acceptance, yet the shadows of bias persist, casting a pall over the lives of many who simply seek love and understanding.

Ageism

While discrimination based on age may be less overt, ageism is a pervasive issue that affects both the young and the elderly. Stereotypes about capability, productivity, and relevance contribute to age-based biases in the workplace and society at large. Unraveling the layers of ageism reveals the nuanced ways in which individuals are unfairly judged and marginalized due to their age, hindering the collective potential of a diverse and intergenerational society.

Ableism

Ableism is discrimination against individuals with disabilities, encompassing prejudiced attitudes, practices, and policies that marginalize or exclude them. It manifests through stereotypes, lack of accessibility, and unequal treatment, requiring efforts to promote inclusivity and challenge discriminatory norms.

Ableism, often overlooked in conversations about discrimination, targets individuals with disabilities. Whether physical or cognitive, those with disabilities face barriers in education, employment, and social integration. The ableist mindset perpetuates a cycle of exclusion, depriving individuals of opportunities and reinforcing harmful stereotypes. An examination of ableism sheds light on the need for inclusivity and accessibility in all facets of life.

Religious Discrimination

Religious discrimination, fueled by deep-seated beliefs and historical conflicts, creates fault lines across societies. Individuals are targeted based on their religious affiliations, leading to discrimination in employment, education, and even violence. The clash of faiths permeates various regions, leaving scars on communities and hindering the prospects for religious harmony.

Economic Discrimination

The socioeconomic divide serves as a breeding ground for economic discrimination, where individuals are judged based on their financial standing. The disparities in access to education, healthcare, and opportunities perpetuate cycles of poverty, reinforcing systemic inequalities. The gulf between the haves and the have-nots widens, creating a stark reminder of the enduring impact of economic discrimination on society.

Conclusion

In reflecting on the dark side of human nature, it becomes evident that bias and discrimination persist across a multitude of societal lines. Racism, sexism, homophobia, ageism, ableism, religious discrimination, and economic discrimination collectively form an intricate web that entraps individuals and communities. To address this ugliness, societies must engage in introspection, fostering empathy, dismantling systemic structures of discrimination, and promoting inclusivity. Only through a concerted effort to confront and eradicate bias can humanity hope to break free from the shackles that bind us and move towards a more equitable and just future.

Chapter 10. From Confidence to Arrogance
The Perils of Overestimating Self-Worth

Introduction

In the intricate landscape of human nature, confidence stands as a virtue that propels individuals towards success and fulfillment. However, the fine line between confidence and arrogance is often blurred, leading to detrimental consequences. This article delves into the transformation from healthy self-assurance to the perilous realm of arrogance, exploring the destructive effects of excessive pride and entitlement.

Understanding the Spectrum

Confidence and arrogance exist on a spectrum, with the former rooted in self-assurance and the latter marked by an inflated sense of superiority. At the outset, confidence is a beacon that guides individuals through challenges, enabling them to navigate life with resilience and poise. It serves as the foundation for personal growth, fostering a positive self-image and a can-do attitude. Yet, the transition from confidence to arrogance occurs when this positive self-perception morphs into an unwarranted sense of entitlement.

The Anatomy of Confidence

Confidence, when genuine, is based on a realistic assessment of one's abilities and achievements. It is grounded in competence, experience, and a healthy acknowledgment of both strengths and weaknesses. Individuals with true confidence are open to learning, receptive to feedback, and capable of adapting to new situations. Confidence empowers individuals to set ambitious goals, pursue challenges, and persevere in the face of setbacks.

The Arrogance Paradox

Arrogance, on the other hand, stems from an overestimation of one's worth and a disregard for others. It creates a distorted perception of self-importance, leading individuals to believe they are superior to those around them. The arrogance paradox lies in the fact that while it may be fueled by an initial sense of confidence, it ultimately undermines personal and interpersonal growth. The arrogant individual becomes resistant to constructive criticism, dismissive of alternative perspectives, and blind to their own shortcomings.

The Destructive Effects of Arrogance

1. Isolation and Alienation

Arrogance fosters an environment of isolation, as the arrogant individual distances themselves from peers, subordinates, and even mentors. The belief in one's inherent superiority leads to a lack of empathy, making genuine connections difficult. This isolation can hinder collaboration, limit support networks, and impede personal and professional development.

2. Stagnation and Complacency

Arrogance blinds individuals to the need for continuous improvement. The assumption of already possessing superior skills and knowledge can breed complacency, stifling innovation and personal development. The arrogant person may rest on past achievements, oblivious to the evolving landscape around them. This stagnation can lead to professional obsolescence and missed opportunities.

3. Strained Relationships

Arrogance erodes the foundations of healthy relationships, both personally and professionally. Constant displays of superiority can breed resentment and animosity among colleagues, friends, and family members. The arrogant individual may struggle to form meaningful connections, as their self-centered attitude alienates those around them.

4. Professional Downfall

In the professional realm, arrogance can be a precursor to downfall. The inability to collaborate effectively, listen to others, and adapt to changing circumstances can lead to poor decision-making and professional setbacks. Colleagues and subordinates may become reluctant to work with an arrogant leader, impacting team dynamics and overall productivity.

5. Emotional Toll

Arrogance, while projecting an image of confidence, often masks deep-seated insecurities. The constant need to assert superiority can take an emotional toll on the individual, leading to stress, anxiety, and a persistent fear of being exposed as a fraud. This emotional turmoil contrasts sharply with the outward display of arrogance, creating an internal conflict that further hinders personal growth.

Recognizing and Mitigating Arrogance

1. Self-Reflection

The first step towards mitigating arrogance is self-reflection. Individuals must objectively assess their attitudes, behaviors, and interactions with others. Honest introspection allows for the identification of arrogant tendencies and provides a foundation for personal growth.

2. Cultivating Humility

Humility serves as a powerful antidote to arrogance. Cultivating an attitude of humility involves acknowledging one's limitations, being receptive to feedback, and recognizing the contributions of others. Embracing a mindset of continuous learning fosters personal and professional development.

3. Seeking Feedback

Actively seeking feedback from peers, mentors, and subordinates is crucial for breaking the cycle of arrogance. Constructive criticism provides valuable insights and helps individuals understand the impact of their behavior on those around them. This openness to feedback is a hallmark of true confidence.

4. Empathy and Perspective-Taking

Developing empathy and the ability to take others' perspectives into account are essential for dismantling arrogance. Understanding the diverse experiences and viewpoints of those around us fosters meaningful connections and promotes a collaborative mindset.

5. Setting Realistic Goals

Arrogance often manifests in unrealistic expectations and grandiose goals. Setting achievable, realistic goals encourages a sense of accomplishment without the need for constant validation. This approach fosters a healthy self-image based on genuine achievements.

Conclusion

The journey from confidence to arrogance is perilous, marked by the erosion of personal and interpersonal well-being. Recognizing the destructive effects of excessive pride and entitlement is essential for fostering a balanced, growth-oriented mindset. By embracing humility, seeking feedback, and cultivating empathy, individuals can navigate the complex terrain of human nature with grace, ensuring that confidence remains a beacon of empowerment rather than a harbinger of downfall. In the reflection on the dark side of human nature, the cautionary tale of arrogance serves as a poignant reminder of the importance of maintaining humility on the path to personal and collective success.

Introduction

In the intricate tapestry of human nature, the concept of the self plays a pivotal role. At the heart of this intricate interplay lies the delicate balance between individuality and empathy. In this exploration of the dark side of human nature, we delve into the Ego Trap, dissecting the fine line that separates healthy self-esteem from the perilous depths of destructive egocentrism.

The Nature of the Ego

To comprehend the Ego Trap, one must first understand the nature of the ego itself. The ego is an integral component of human psychology, representing an individual's sense of self. Rooted in self-awareness, it is the lens through which we perceive ourselves in relation to the world. While a healthy ego fosters confidence and self-assurance, it is essential to recognize the potential for it to morph into a source of destructive behavior.

The Allure of Healthy Self-Esteem

Healthy self-esteem is the cornerstone of a well-balanced psyche. It empowers individuals to navigate life's challenges with confidence, resilience, and a positive outlook. A strong sense of self-worth enables us to pursue our goals, form meaningful connections, and contribute positively to society. The challenge lies in maintaining this healthy equilibrium without succumbing to the gravitational pull of unchecked egocentrism.

Crossing the Threshold

The transition from healthy self-esteem to destructive egocentrism often occurs insidiously. As individuals gain accolades, recognition, or power, the ego may begin to swell. This escalation, if left unchecked, can lead to a distorted sense of superiority, where empathy and understanding for others are overshadowed by a singular focus on personal gratification. The Ego Trap tightens its grip as the individual becomes increasingly absorbed in their own narrative.

Narcissism

At the extreme end of the egocentric spectrum lies narcissism, a personality trait characterized by an exaggerated sense of self-importance, a constant need for admiration, and a lack of empathy for others. Narcissism represents the darker manifestation of the ego, where the individual's insatiable desire for self-aggrandizement eclipses any consideration for the feelings or needs of those around them.

The Erosion of Empathy

As the ego swells, empathy tends to erode. The ability to understand and share the feelings of others takes a backseat to the relentless pursuit of self-interest. This erosion of empathy not only strains personal relationships but can have profound societal implications, fostering a culture of individualism at the expense of collective well-being.

Social Ramifications of Ego-driven Behavior

In a world increasingly interconnected, ego-driven behavior reverberates beyond individual lives. From workplaces to communities, the toxic influence of unchecked egocentrism can lead to a breakdown in communication, collaboration, and the fabric of social harmony. Identifying and addressing these societal ramifications is crucial in mitigating the dark side of human nature.

Cultivating Empathy

To escape the clutches of the Ego Trap, individuals must actively cultivate empathy. This involves recognizing the humanity in others, practicing active listening, and developing a genuine understanding of diverse perspectives. Empathy serves as the counterbalance to ego-driven behavior, fostering compassion, cooperation, and the building of meaningful connections.

The Role of Self-Reflection

Central to the journey of escaping the Ego Trap is the practice of self-reflection. Individuals must engage in honest introspection, scrutinizing their motives, actions, and their impact on those around them. This self-awareness serves as a powerful tool in dismantling the illusions of unchecked egocentrism and fostering personal growth.

Humility as an Antidote

Humility stands as the antidote to the poison of ego-driven behavior. Embracing humility involves acknowledging one's limitations, recognizing the contributions of others, and approaching life with a genuine openness to learning. By cultivating humility, individuals can break free from the confines of the Ego Trap and foster a more harmonious existence.

The Power of Collective Empathy

While individual efforts are crucial, addressing the dark side of human nature requires a collective commitment to empathy. Societal structures, educational systems, and cultural norms must encourage the development of empathy as a core value. By nurturing a collective sense of understanding and compassion, we can create a world where the Ego Trap holds less sway over our shared destiny.

Conclusion

The journey through the Ego Trap is a complex exploration of the self and its relationship with others. Striking a balance between individuality and empathy is a perpetual challenge, and the consequences of failure are significant. By understanding the nature of the ego, recognizing the signs of egocentrism, and actively cultivating empathy, individuals can navigate this delicate equilibrium, contributing to a more compassionate and interconnected world. In the reflections on the dark side of human nature, the Ego Trap serves as a poignant reminder of the constant need for self-awareness, humility, and a collective commitment to fostering empathy in the human experience.

Chapter 12. Green-Eyed Monsters
Jealousy and Envy in Everyday Life

Introduction

In the complex tapestry of human emotions, jealousy and envy stand out as potent forces that can shape our thoughts, actions, and relationships. These green-eyed monsters lurk in the shadows of our psyche, revealing the darker aspects of human nature. This article delves into the intricacies of jealousy and envy, exploring their psychological underpinnings, their impact on individuals, and the broader social consequences they can unleash.

Understanding Jealousy and Envy

Jealousy and envy are often used interchangeably, but they represent distinct emotional experiences. Jealousy typically arises from the fear of losing something valuable, be it a relationship, status, or possession, to a perceived rival. Envy, on the other hand, emerges when one desires something possessed by another, harboring resentment for their advantage.

Psychological Roots of Jealousy and Envy

1. Evolutionary Perspectives

Jealousy and envy have evolutionary roots, playing a role in the survival of the fittest. In the ancestral environment, competition for resources and mates was fierce. These emotions may have evolved as mechanisms to motivate individuals to protect and secure what is essential for their survival and reproduction.

2. Social Comparison Theory

Psychologist Leon Festinger's Social Comparison Theory posits that individuals evaluate their abilities and opinions by comparing themselves to others. When the comparison reveals a perceived disadvantage, jealousy or envy may arise, influencing self-esteem and emotional well-being.

Impact on Individuals

1. Emotional Turmoil

Jealousy and envy can plunge individuals into a whirlwind of negative emotions. The fear of inadequacy, the pain of perceived betrayal, and the bitterness of unfulfilled desires can lead to stress, anxiety, and even depression.

2. Relationship Strain

In intimate relationships, jealousy can erode trust and create an atmosphere of suspicion. Envy, when left unchecked, may breed resentment, causing distance between individuals. Both emotions can be toxic to the fabric of relationships, leading to conflicts and, in extreme cases, separation.

3. Self-Esteem Challenges

Constant comparison with others, fueled by envy, can take a toll on one's self-esteem. The relentless pursuit of unattainable standards set by others can lead to feelings of inadequacy and unworthiness.

Social Consequences of Envy

1. Undermining Cooperation

Envy within social groups can undermine cooperation and collaboration. When individuals feel resentful of others' success, they may be less inclined to work together towards common goals. This can hinder progress and create a divisive atmosphere.

2. Economic Inequality

Envy can contribute to the perpetuation of economic inequality. The desire for material success and social status, coupled with resentment towards those who have achieved it, can lead to a cycle of competition that exacerbates societal disparities.

3. Impact on Mental Health

The prevalence of envy in a society can contribute to a collective decline in mental health. Constant comparison and the pursuit of unrealistic standards can create a culture of anxiety and dissatisfaction, affecting the overall well-being of individuals.

Coping Mechanisms and Mitigation

1. Self-awareness

Recognizing and acknowledging one's feelings of jealousy and envy is the first step towards managing these emotions. Understanding the source of these feelings can empower individuals to address the underlying issues.

2. Cultivating Gratitude

Fostering a mindset of gratitude can counteract the negative effects of envy. By focusing on one's blessings and achievements, individuals can shift their perspective and find contentment in what they have rather than what they lack.

3. Building Empathy

Developing empathy towards others' successes and challenges can foster a more compassionate and understanding attitude. Recognizing that everyone faces their own struggles can diminish the intensity of envy and promote a sense of shared humanity.

Conclusion

Jealousy and envy, though deeply rooted in human nature, are not insurmountable forces. By understanding their psychological origins and societal consequences, individuals can take proactive steps to mitigate their impact. Through self-awareness, empathy, and a commitment to building positive relationships, we can strive to keep the green-eyed monsters at bay and cultivate a healthier, more harmonious existence. In reflecting on the dark side of human nature, we find opportunities for growth, resilience, and the pursuit of a more compassionate society.

Chapter 13. The Intolerance Paradox
Navigating Diversity in a Globalized World

Introduction

In an era marked by unprecedented connectivity and globalization, the concept of tolerance takes center stage as societies grapple with the complexities of diversity. The paradoxical nature of intolerance, often hidden beneath the surface of seemingly harmonious interactions, becomes a critical aspect of the human experience. This article explores the challenges of fostering tolerance in our interconnected world, delving into the intricacies of the intolerance paradox.

Understanding the Intolerance Paradox

The intolerance paradox is a phenomenon where the very openness and diversity that characterize a globalized society can give rise to intolerance. As communities become more interconnected, the clash of diverse values, beliefs, and cultures can fuel tensions and animosities. This paradox highlights the challenge of maintaining tolerance in the face of increasing diversity and the need to navigate through the dark side of human nature.

The Illusion of Homogeneity

In a globalized world, the illusion of homogeneity often conceals deep-seated prejudices. As societies become more interconnected, the expectation of a harmonious blend of cultures can inadvertently lead to the suppression of individual identities. The pressure to conform to a perceived global norm can create an environment where diversity is tolerated only on the surface, masking underlying biases that simmer beneath.

Digital Echo Chambers and Polarization

The digital age has revolutionized the way information is disseminated, but it has also given rise to echo chambers that reinforce pre-existing beliefs. While social media connects people across the globe, it can also amplify divisions by creating isolated communities that only interact with like-minded individuals. This digital polarization intensifies intolerance as people become entrenched in their viewpoints, closing themselves off to alternative perspectives.

Erosion of Cultural Relativism

Cultural relativism is the perspective that beliefs, customs, and values are best understood and evaluated within the context of their own culture rather than being judged by the standards of another. Cultural relativism faces challenges in a globalized world. The clash of cultures often erodes this relativistic approach, with one culture imposing its values on another. The danger lies in the loss of cultural diversity as dominant ideologies overshadow indigenous beliefs, contributing to the intolerance paradox.

Economic Disparities and Social Injustice

Globalization has brought economic opportunities, but it has also widened the gap between the privileged and the marginalized. Economic disparities often translate into social injustice, fostering resentment and intolerance. The intolerance paradox manifests as societies fail to address the root causes of inequality, allowing prejudices to thrive in the fertile ground of discontent.

Education as a Double-Edged Sword

Education, while essential for fostering tolerance, can inadvertently contribute to the intolerance paradox. A standardized curriculum may propagate a biased version of history, marginalizing certain cultures and perpetuating stereotypes. Additionally, the education system itself can become a breeding ground for intolerance if it fails to promote critical thinking and open-mindedness.

The Role of Political Leadership

Political leaders play a pivotal role in either exacerbating or mitigating the intolerance paradox. Leaders who exploit divisions for political gain contribute to the erosion of social cohesion. On the other hand, leaders who champion inclusivity and diversity can pave the way for a more tolerant society. Political decisions and policies shape the narrative of a nation, influencing the degree to which intolerance is allowed to flourish.

Building Bridges through Dialogue

Dialogue becomes a powerful tool in breaking down the walls of intolerance. Meaningful conversations that transcend cultural, religious, and ideological boundaries are essential for fostering understanding. Creating spaces where individuals can engage in open and respectful discussions is crucial in dismantling the intolerance paradox. Dialogue promotes empathy, helping individuals recognize the shared humanity that unites us all.

Empowering Local Initiatives

While global initiatives are important, empowering local communities to address intolerance is equally crucial. Grassroots movements that celebrate diversity and inclusivity at the community level can have a profound impact. Local initiatives have the advantage of understanding the unique dynamics of their communities, tailoring interventions to address specific challenges and bridge divides.

Media Literacy for the 21st Century

Media literacy emerges as a critical component in navigating the intolerance paradox. Teaching individuals to critically analyze information, recognize biases, and discern misinformation is essential in the digital age. By fostering media literacy, societies can equip individuals with the tools to navigate the complex web of information, promoting a more informed and tolerant citizenry.

Conclusion

The intolerance paradox poses a formidable challenge in an interconnected world where diversity is both a source of enrichment and a potential breeding ground for discord. Recognizing the intricacies of this paradox is the first step towards fostering tolerance. By addressing the illusion of homogeneity, navigating digital echo chambers, upholding cultural relativism, tackling economic disparities, reforming education, and promoting inclusive dialogue, societies can work towards dismantling the intolerance paradox. It is through these concerted efforts, both global and local, that we can aspire to create a world where diversity is not merely tolerated but celebrated as a testament to the richness of the human experience.

Introduction

In the intricate tapestry of human nature, there exists a dark thread that weaves its way through society, leaving behind a trail of shattered trust and emotional turmoil. Theft, a crime as old as civilization itself, has profound implications for individuals and the broader community. This article delves into the multifaceted impact of theft, exploring the emotional and societal repercussions that reverberate through the lives of those affected.

Betrayal of Trust

At its core, theft is a betrayal of trust. Whether it's a pickpocket snatching a wallet, a corporate executive embezzling funds, or a friend stealing from another, the act undermines the foundation of trust that binds individuals and communities together. Trust, once stolen, becomes a fragile entity that takes time to rebuild. The emotional toll on victims is immeasurable, as they grapple with feelings of violation, vulnerability, and betrayal.

1. Emotional Turmoil

Violation of Personal Space

The act of theft violates the sanctity of personal space, turning what should be a haven into a breeding ground for insecurity. Victims often experience a profound sense of violation, as their belongings, whether tangible or intangible, are forcibly taken from them. The emotional wounds inflicted by this violation linger long after the physical loss is repaired.

Erosion of Security

Theft erodes the sense of security that individuals have in their surroundings. The once-assumed safety of one's home or workplace is replaced by a constant undercurrent of fear and suspicion. Victims find themselves questioning the intentions of those around them, fostering a sense of paranoia that can be challenging to overcome.

2. Trust Issues

Distrust of Others

Having experienced the betrayal of theft, individuals often develop a heightened distrust of others. Friends, family, and even strangers are viewed through a lens colored by suspicion, making it difficult to form genuine connections. The ripple effect of this distrust extends beyond personal relationships, influencing how individuals engage with society at large.

Impact on Interpersonal Relationships

The emotional fallout from theft can strain interpersonal relationships. Friends may distance themselves, unsure of how to navigate the newfound tension, and family dynamics may be forever altered. Rebuilding trust becomes an uphill battle, as victims struggle to reconcile the betrayal with their previous perceptions of those they once held dear.

Societal Ramifications

The impact of theft extends beyond individual experiences, permeating the fabric of society and contributing to broader issues that compromise communal well-being.

1. Economic Consequences

Financial Strain

Theft often results in immediate financial strain for individuals and businesses alike. Whether it's the loss of personal savings or the depletion of company resources, the economic repercussions are felt acutely. For many, the aftermath of theft involves navigating the arduous path of financial recovery, further exacerbating stress and anxiety.

Increased Security Measures

As a response to rising theft rates, societies implement heightened security measures. Businesses invest in surveillance systems, individuals resort to safeguarding their belongings through locks and alarms, and communities become more vigilant. While these measures aim to deter theft, they also contribute to a pervasive atmosphere of suspicion and surveillance.

2. Erosion of Social Cohesion

Fragmentation of Trust

The prevalence of theft within a society erodes the collective trust that binds communities together. When individuals perceive a lack of security and trustworthiness in their surroundings, the social fabric begins to unravel. This fragmentation can lead to increased isolation, as people withdraw from communal activities and interactions.

Impact on Social Equality

Theft disproportionately affects vulnerable populations, exacerbating existing social inequalities. Those with fewer resources are more susceptible to financial devastation, widening the gap between the privileged and the marginalized. The resulting disparities contribute to a fractured society where trust becomes a luxury afforded to the few.

The Cycle of Recidivism

Examining the impact of theft necessitates an exploration of the cyclical nature of criminal behavior. Recidivism, the tendency for individuals to relapse into criminal activities after punishment or rehabilitation, perpetuates the negative consequences of theft on both individuals and society.

1. Psychological Factors

Root Causes of Criminal Behavior

Understanding the root causes of theft is crucial in addressing recidivism. Psychological factors such as poverty, substance abuse, and a lack of education often contribute to criminal behavior. Addressing these underlying issues is essential for breaking the cycle of theft and fostering rehabilitation.

Rehabilitation Programs

Investing in rehabilitation programs that address the psychological and social factors associated with theft can be a proactive approach to mitigating recidivism. These programs should focus on skill development, mental health support, and community reintegration, offering individuals a chance to rebuild their lives.

2. Breaking the Cycle

Education and Empowerment

Breaking the cycle of theft requires a multifaceted approach, with education playing a pivotal role. Empowering individuals with the knowledge and skills necessary to escape the cycle of poverty and crime is essential for creating lasting change. Access to education and vocational training can provide alternatives to a life of theft.

Community Support

Communities must play an active role in supporting individuals who have committed theft but are seeking rehabilitation. Embracing a more compassionate and understanding approach can contribute to the reintegration of these individuals into society, breaking the cycle of recidivism and fostering a sense of collective responsibility.

Conclusion

Stealing trust through acts of theft has far-reaching consequences, impacting individuals emotionally and contributing to societal challenges. The betrayal of trust leaves emotional scars that persist long after the physical losses have been replaced. On a broader scale, theft undermines the social cohesion that binds communities together, perpetuating cycles of distrust and inequality. Understanding the root causes of theft and implementing rehabilitation programs are crucial steps toward breaking the cycle of recidivism and fostering a society built on trust and empathy. As we reflect on the dark side of human nature, it becomes imperative to address the impact of theft with a holistic approach that combines individual healing with societal transformation.

Chapter 15. White-Collar Crimes
Unraveling the Web of Financial Deceit

Introduction

The term "white-collar crime" was coined by sociologist Edwin Sutherland in 1939, referring to non-violent crimes committed by individuals, businesses, or government professionals in their pursuit of financial gain. These crimes often involve deceit, manipulation, and abuse of trust, leaving a trail of financial ruin and shattered lives. In this article, we will delve into the intricate world of white-collar crimes, exploring their nature, impact, and the challenges of investigating and prosecuting those responsible.

Defining White-Collar Crimes

White-collar crimes encompass a wide range of offenses, including fraud, embezzlement, insider trading, money laundering, and corporate misconduct. Unlike traditional crimes, these offenses are committed by individuals in positions of trust, often exploiting their authority to achieve financial gain without resorting to physical force. Understanding the nuances of these crimes is crucial for unraveling the web of financial deceit.

The Faces of Deception

1. Corporate Fraud

One of the most prevalent forms of white-collar crime is corporate fraud, where executives manipulate financial statements, inflate earnings, or engage in other deceptive practices to portray a false image of a company's financial health. The fallout from corporate fraud can be catastrophic, leading to stock market crashes, job losses, and widespread economic turmoil.

2. Insider Trading

Insider trading involves trading stocks based on confidential, non-public information. Corporate insiders, such as executives or employees, may exploit their privileged position to gain an unfair advantage in the stock market. This illicit practice undermines the integrity of financial markets and erodes public trust in the fairness of the system.

The Impact on Society

1. Economic Consequences

White-collar crimes have far-reaching consequences that extend beyond the immediate victims. The economic impact can be profound, as investors lose faith in financial institutions, markets become volatile, and businesses suffer from the fallout. The 2008 financial crisis, fueled by corporate malfeasance, is a stark example of the devastating repercussions of unchecked white-collar crime.

2. Trust Erosion

White-collar crimes erode the trust that underpins societal institutions. When individuals in positions of authority exploit their power for personal gain, it breeds cynicism and skepticism, shaking the foundations of trust that bind communities together. Rebuilding this trust becomes a monumental task, requiring both legal and societal interventions.

Investigating White-Collar Crimes

1. Complex Nature

Investigating white-collar crimes is inherently challenging due to their complex and sophisticated nature. Unlike traditional crimes with visible evidence, financial deceit often leaves a trail of intricate transactions, obscured by layers of complexity. Investigators must navigate this labyrinth to uncover the truth.

2. Regulatory Framework

In the United States, effective investigation of white-collar crimes relies on a robust regulatory framework. Government agencies, such as the Securities and Exchange Commission (SEC) and the Federal Bureau of Investigation (FBI), play a crucial role in monitoring and regulating financial activities. Strengthening these regulatory bodies is essential for preventing and combating white-collar crimes.

Legal Challenges in Prosecution

1. Burden of Proof

Prosecuting white-collar criminals presents unique challenges, primarily due to the burden of proof. Establishing guilt often requires demonstrating intent, a task complicated by the subtleties of financial transactions. Legal systems must adapt to address these challenges, ensuring that perpetrators are held accountable for their actions.

2. Corporate Accountability

Holdings corporations accountable for the actions of their executives poses a significant legal challenge. Establishing corporate liability requires proving that the organization had knowledge of, or was complicit in, the criminal activities. Striking a balance between punishing corporate wrongdoing and safeguarding innocent stakeholders is an ongoing legal conundrum.

Emerging Trends in White-Collar Crimes

1. Cybercrime and Technology

As technology advances, so do the methods employed by white-collar criminals. Cybercrime, including hacking, identity theft, and online fraud, has become a prevalent avenue for financial deception. Law enforcement agencies must continually adapt to these evolving tactics to stay ahead of the curve.

2. Globalization and Transnational Crimes

The interconnected nature of the global economy has facilitated the rise of transnational white-collar crimes. Money laundering, tax evasion, and bribery often involve complex networks that span multiple jurisdictions. International cooperation and coordination among law enforcement agencies are essential to combat these sophisticated crimes effectively.

The Psychology of White-Collar Criminals

1. Rationalization and Justification

Rationalization is a defense mechanism where individuals provide logical or reasonable explanations for actions or decisions that are actually based on irrational or emotional factors. It often involves self-deception to make an undesirable situation or behavior seem more acceptable. *Justification* involves providing valid reasons or evidence to support a particular decision or action. Unlike rationalization, justification may or may not involve self-deception, as individuals can offer sound and objective reasons for their choices.

Understanding the psychology of white-collar criminals is vital for prevention and rehabilitation. Many offenders engage in rationalization and justification, convincing themselves that their actions are morally acceptable or necessary. Exploring the psychological underpinnings of these behaviors can inform efforts to address the root causes of white-collar crime.

2. Narcissism and Hubris

Narcissism is a personality trait characterized by a grandiose sense of self-importance, a preoccupation with fantasies of unlimited success, power, beauty, or ideal love, and a lack of empathy for others. *Hubris* refers to excessive pride, arrogance, or overconfidence, often leading to a lack of respect for others or for the natural order of things. It involves an inflated sense of one's abilities or accomplishments.

Traits such as narcissism and hubris are often prevalent among white-collar criminals. The belief in one's superiority and entitlement can lead individuals to engage in risky and unethical behavior, underestimating the potential consequences. Recognizing and addressing these personality traits can contribute to preventive measures.

Conclusion

White-collar crimes represent a dark facet of human nature, where individuals entrusted with power and responsibility succumb to greed and deceit. Unraveling the web of financial deceit requires a multifaceted approach, encompassing legal, regulatory, and societal interventions. As we reflect on the dark side of human nature, it becomes imperative to address the root causes, strengthen regulatory frameworks, and foster a culture of transparency and accountability to prevent and combat white-collar crimes. Only through collective efforts can we hope to dismantle the intricate webs woven by those who exploit trust for personal gain.

Introduction

In the complex tapestry of human nature, there exists a thread that often goes unnoticed but casts a dark shadow upon society - apathy. Apathy, characterized by a lack of interest, enthusiasm, or concern, has far-reaching consequences that permeate every aspect of human interaction. This article delves into the depths of apathy, exploring its roots, manifestations, and the profound societal implications of widespread indifference.

The Roots of Apathy

1. Psychological Underpinnings

Apathy often finds its roots in the intricate web of human psychology. Theories suggest that repeated exposure to overwhelming stressors, coupled with a sense of powerlessness, can lead individuals to retreat into apathy as a coping mechanism. The constant barrage of information and stimuli in the modern world can also contribute to emotional exhaustion, rendering individuals desensitized and indifferent.

2. Societal Factors

Societal structures can play a pivotal role in breeding apathy. Economic disparities, systemic injustices, and a lack of social cohesion can create an environment where individuals feel disconnected from the collective well-being. When people perceive their efforts as futile in the face of systemic issues, they may succumb to apathy, resigning themselves to a passive existence.

Manifestations of Apathy

1. Political Apathy

One of the most evident manifestations of apathy is found in the realm of politics. Widespread disinterest in civic participation, low voter turnout, and a lack of engagement with public affairs can result in a weakened democracy. When individuals feel that their voices hold no weight, political apathy becomes a breeding ground for manipulation and a decline in the overall health of democratic institutions.

2. Environmental Apathy

The environment, facing unprecedented challenges, is another battleground for apathy. Indifference towards ecological concerns can lead to unsustainable practices, overexploitation of natural resources, and a reluctance to address climate change. The consequences of environmental apathy are not only felt by the planet but also by future generations who inherit the repercussions of our collective indifference.

3. Social Apathy

On a more personal level, apathy infiltrates interpersonal relationships. The decline of empathy and a lack of emotional investment can strain social bonds, leading to isolation and a breakdown of community connections. The erosion of compassion and understanding in the face of societal challenges further exacerbates the consequences of social apathy.

Societal Implications

1. Erosion of Social Fabric

Apathy acts as a corrosive force, gradually eroding the social fabric that binds communities together. When individuals become indifferent to the struggles of their fellow citizens, the sense of shared responsibility diminishes. This erosion of social bonds leaves society vulnerable to fragmentation, fostering an environment where collective action becomes increasingly elusive.

2. Weakening of Democratic Values

In the political sphere, the consequences of apathy extend beyond mere disinterest. Apathy weakens the very foundations of democratic values by diminishing civic engagement. When a significant portion of the population abstains from participating in the democratic process, the risk of authoritarianism or the exploitation of political power increases, leading to a society that fails to uphold the principles it was built upon.

3. Environmental Degradation

The consequences of environmental apathy reverberate across the globe. From deforestation to pollution, the lack of collective concern for the environment hastens the degradation of ecosystems. The long-term impacts on biodiversity, climate, and natural resources pose a direct threat to the well-being of present and future generations, underscoring the urgent need for a shift away from apathy towards proactive environmental stewardship.

Overcoming Apathy: A Call to Action

1. Cultivating Empathy

At the heart of combating apathy lies the cultivation of empathy. Encouraging individuals to understand and relate to the experiences of others fosters a sense of shared humanity. By actively promoting empathy, societies can counteract the detachment that fuels apathy, nurturing a collective spirit that values compassion and mutual support.

2. Fostering Civic Engagement

To address political apathy, efforts must be made to foster civic engagement. Education plays a crucial role in empowering individuals with the knowledge and tools needed to participate meaningfully in the democratic process. Encouraging open dialogue and creating platforms for informed discussion can rekindle interest in political affairs and strengthen the democratic foundation.

3. Environmental Consciousness

Combatting environmental apathy requires a fundamental shift in the way societies perceive and interact with the natural world. Promoting environmental education, sustainable practices, and policies that prioritize ecological well-being can instill a sense of responsibility towards the planet. Recognizing the interconnectedness of human existence with the environment is vital for fostering a collective commitment to sustainable living.

Conclusion

The exploration of apathy unveils the intricate interplay between individual psychology and societal structures. The consequences of apathy are profound, reaching into the realms of politics, the environment, and interpersonal relationships. However, this exploration is not merely a grim portrayal of human nature but a call to action. By understanding the roots of apathy and actively working towards cultivating empathy, fostering civic engagement, and promoting environmental consciousness, societies can break free from the chains of indifference and pave the way for a more compassionate and engaged world.

Introduction

In the vast landscape of human nature, the emergence of the digital age has cast a shadow that extends beyond the physical realm. As our lives become increasingly intertwined with technology, so too does the darker side of human nature find new avenues of expression. The digital realm, with its promise of connectivity and progress, has also become a breeding ground for cyber shadows – the unseen crimes that lurk in the dark corners of the internet. This article delves into the prevalence and impact of online crimes, examining the multifaceted nature of cyber shadows.

The Evolution of Cybercrime

The advent of the internet brought about a revolutionary shift in the way we communicate, work, and conduct business. However, as the digital landscape expanded, so did the opportunities for criminal activities. Cybercrime, once a term reserved for a niche of computer enthusiasts with malicious intent, has evolved into a sophisticated and widespread threat. From hackers seeking financial gain to state-sponsored cyber-espionage, the spectrum of cybercriminal activities has broadened, leaving a trail of victims in its wake.

The Faceless Adversaries

Unlike traditional crimes where perpetrators often operate within a tangible environment, cybercriminals exist in the shadows of anonymity. The faceless nature of these adversaries makes it challenging for law enforcement to track and apprehend them. Operating under pseudonyms (fictitious names or aliases used by individuals to conceal their real identities) and utilizing advanced technologies to conceal their identities, these digital criminals exploit the very anonymity that the internet was designed to provide.

Financial Implications

One of the most tangible impacts of cyber shadows is the financial toll it takes on individuals, businesses, and even nations. Cybercriminals employ a variety of tactics, such as phishing, ransomware attacks, and identity theft, to siphon off funds or demand hefty ransoms. The financial losses incurred by victims extend beyond the immediate material impact, often causing long-term economic repercussions and eroding trust in online transactions.

The Weaponization of Information

In the digital age, information has become a powerful weapon wielded by those with malicious intent. Disinformation campaigns, hacking of critical infrastructure, and cyber-espionage have become prevalent tactics employed by state and non-state actors alike. The weaponization of information not only threatens national security but also undermines the very fabric of trust that holds societies together.

Psychological Toll

Beyond the tangible losses, cyber shadows cast a psychological toll on individuals and communities. The fear of falling victim to cybercrime, the erosion of privacy, and the constant threat of online harassment contribute to a pervasive sense of insecurity. The digital age, which promised to bring people closer, has paradoxically left many feeling exposed and vulnerable.

The Challenge of Attribution

Attributing cybercrimes to specific individuals or entities remains a significant challenge. The use of sophisticated techniques to conceal identities, coupled with the global nature of the internet, makes it difficult for authorities to trace the origins of cyber attacks accurately. This lack of attribution not only emboldens cybercriminals but also hampers international efforts to combat online crimes effectively.

Legal and Ethical Dilemmas

The digital age has presented legal and ethical dilemmas that lawmakers and society at large are still grappling with. Questions surrounding jurisdiction, the definition of cybercrimes, and the appropriate punishment for offenders remain unresolved. The rapid evolution of technology often outpaces the development of legal frameworks, leaving a gap that cybercriminals exploit.

The Role of Technology in Combating Cyber Shadows

While technology has been an enabler of cybercrime, it also holds the key to combating the growing menace of cyber shadows. Advancements in artificial intelligence, machine learning, and cybersecurity tools empower individuals and organizations to detect and prevent cyber threats. The collaboration between technology experts, law enforcement agencies, and policymakers becomes crucial in staying one step ahead of cybercriminals.

Building Resilience in the Digital Age

As societies navigate the digital landscape, building resilience against cyber shadows becomes imperative. This involves a multi-faceted approach, including education on cybersecurity best practices, the development of robust legal frameworks, and international collaboration to tackle cross-border cybercrimes. Individuals and organizations must become proactive in securing their digital presence to mitigate the risks posed by cyber shadows.

Conclusion

This chapter on Cyber Shadows reveals a complex tapestry of crimes in the digital age. From the faceless adversaries who operate in the shadows to the far-reaching consequences on individuals and societies, the impact of cybercrime is profound. As we grapple with the challenges posed by cyber shadows, it becomes clear that addressing the darker aspects of human nature in the digital age requires a concerted effort from individuals, communities, and nations. Only through understanding, collaboration, and the responsible use of technology can we hope to dispel the shadows that loom over the digital landscape and usher in an era of greater security and trust.

Introduction

In the seemingly mundane routine of daily life, public spaces often become battlegrounds for women, who find themselves navigating through the dark underbelly of human nature - street harassment. Beyond the seemingly harmless catcalls lie the harsh realities of a pervasive issue that plagues women worldwide. This article delves into the multifaceted nature of street harassment, exploring its origins, impact, and the urgent need for societal change.

Defining Street Harassment

Catcalling refers to the act of making loud, often sexually suggestive, and unwanted remarks or gestures, typically directed at someone in a public space, often a stranger. It is a form of street harassment that can make individuals feel uncomfortable, objectified, or unsafe. Catcalling is widely criticized as disrespectful and contributes to the broader issue of gender-based harassment.

Leering refers to the act of looking at someone in an unpleasant, predatory, or suggestive manner, often with a facial expression that indicates lust or desire. It involves a prolonged and often intrusive gaze that can make the person being looked at feel uncomfortable, objectified, or harassed. Leering is considered disrespectful and can contribute to an unwelcome or threatening atmosphere, particularly in the context of sexual harassment.

Street harassment encompasses a spectrum of unwelcome behaviors, from catcalling and leering to unwanted advances and physical intimidation. It is a manifestation of gender-based violence, reinforcing power imbalances and perpetuating the societal subjugation of women. The overt nature of catcalling often serves as the tip of the iceberg, overshadowing the subtler yet equally insidious forms of harassment that women endure daily.

The Psychological Toll

Street harassment extends far beyond the momentary discomfort of a catcall. The cumulative psychological toll on women is profound, contributing to feelings of anxiety, fear, and vulnerability. The constant vigilance required to navigate public spaces restricts women's freedom, limiting their ability to move freely without the specter of harassment looming over them. The normalization of such behavior perpetuates a culture of silence, where victims often internalize their trauma, compounding the emotional impact.

Unraveling the Roots

To comprehend the issue at its core, it is imperative to unravel the roots of street harassment. This behavior is deeply entrenched in patriarchal structures that perpetuate gender inequalities. The power dynamics inherent in a society that objectifies and commodifies women create an environment where harassment thrives. Addressing street harassment requires dismantling these ingrained structures, challenging toxic masculinity, and fostering a culture of respect and equality.

Impact on Women's Lives

The repercussions of street harassment extend beyond the immediate emotional distress. Women often alter their routines and behaviors to avoid potential harassment, restricting their mobility and hindering their access to public spaces. This has broader implications, affecting women's professional and social lives. The fear of harassment can deter women from pursuing certain careers, hobbies, or even exercising their right to leisure.

The Role of Catcalling

While catcalling is just one manifestation of street harassment, its prevalence makes it a focal point of discussion. Catcalls are not harmless compliments; they are a display of power, objectification, and entitlement. The seemingly innocuous act of shouting comments about a woman's appearance serves to reinforce societal norms that prioritize male desires over female autonomy. Understanding catcalling as a gateway to more severe forms of harassment is crucial in developing effective strategies to combat street harassment.

Intersectionality and Street Harassment

Street harassment is not a one-size-fits-all experience. Intersectionality plays a significant role, as individuals may face varying degrees of harassment based on their race, ethnicity, sexual orientation, or socioeconomic status. Women of color, LGBTQ+ individuals, and those from marginalized communities often endure additional layers of discrimination, compounding the challenges they face in public spaces. An inclusive approach to addressing street harassment must recognize and combat these intersecting forms of oppression.

The Role of Bystanders

The responsibility of combatting street harassment does not rest solely on the shoulders of those directly affected. Bystanders play a crucial role in challenging and changing societal norms. The prevalence of a bystander effect, where individuals hesitate to intervene or speak out, allows harassment to persist unchecked. Encouraging bystander intervention programs and fostering a culture of accountability are essential steps toward creating safer public spaces.

Legal Measures and Enforcement

While societal change is vital, legal measures and enforcement mechanisms also play a crucial role in addressing street harassment. Many jurisdictions have recognized the severity of the issue and implemented legislation to combat harassment in public spaces. However, the effectiveness of these measures often depends on robust enforcement, education, and an understanding of the nuanced nature of street harassment.

Educational Initiatives

Addressing street harassment requires a comprehensive educational approach. Initiatives aimed at raising awareness about the impact of harassment, promoting consent education, and challenging traditional gender norms are crucial. Educational institutions, community organizations, and public campaigns can all contribute to fostering a culture that rejects harassment and promotes respect for all individuals.

Empowering Survivors

Empowering survivors of street harassment involves creating safe spaces for them to share their experiences, seek support, and be heard. Breaking the culture of silence and shame is essential in dismantling the cycle of harassment. Support systems, counseling services, and community outreach programs can aid in the healing process and empower survivors to reclaim their agency.

Conclusion

Street harassment is a dark manifestation of human nature that thrives in the shadows of gender inequality. Beyond the surface-level catcalls lies a complex web of power dynamics, societal norms, and ingrained behaviors that perpetuate this pervasive issue. Understanding the roots, impact, and intersectionality of street harassment is essential in developing effective strategies for change. It is a collective responsibility to challenge toxic norms, empower survivors, and create a society where public spaces are safe for everyone, irrespective of gender or identity. Only through a concerted effort can we hope to illuminate the dark side of human nature and pave the way for a future free from the shackles of street harassment.

Introduction

The shadowed corners of human nature often harbor some of the most profound struggles individuals face. Addiction, a formidable adversary, casts a pervasive and enduring shadow, affecting millions of lives worldwide. In this exploration of the dark side of human nature, we delve into the complexities of addiction, unraveling its intricate web and shedding light on the societal impact it leaves in its wake.

The Nature of Addiction

1. Defining Addiction

At its core, addiction is a chronic, relapsing disorder characterized by compulsive seeking, continued use, and a lack of control despite adverse consequences. Whether rooted in substance abuse or behavioral patterns, addiction hijacks the brain's reward system, rewiring neural pathways and fostering a cycle of dependence.

2. The Neurobiology of Addiction

Understanding addiction necessitates an exploration of its neurobiological underpinnings. Dopamine, a neurotransmitter associated with pleasure and reward, plays a central role. The hijacking of the brain's reward circuitry alters decision-making processes and reinforces the addictive behavior, perpetuating a self-destructive cycle.

Breaking the Chains

1. Acknowledging the Problem

The journey to recovery begins with acknowledging the presence of addiction. Whether self-awareness or prompted by external interventions, this initial step sets the stage for an individual's commitment to change.

2. Seeking Support

Breaking free from the chains of addiction seldom occurs in isolation. Support networks, comprising friends, family, and professionals, provide crucial pillars of strength. Therapy, counseling, and support groups offer avenues for individuals to confront their struggles and build resilience.

3. Treatment Modalities

Various treatment modalities exist to address addiction, tailored to the specific needs of individuals. From medical interventions to psychotherapy, the spectrum of options reflects the multifaceted nature of addiction. Rehabilitation programs, detoxification, and medication-assisted therapies contribute to a comprehensive approach to recovery.

The Societal Impact of Addiction

1. Family Dynamics

The repercussions of addiction extend far beyond the individual grappling with the disorder. Families bear a significant burden as they navigate the challenges of living with a loved one in the throes of addiction. Trust is eroded, relationships strained, and the emotional toll can be devastating.

2. Economic Implications

Society at large also shoulders the economic burden of addiction. Lost productivity, healthcare costs, and criminal justice expenses contribute to a substantial financial toll. Addressing addiction requires a holistic approach that considers both the personal and societal dimensions of this multifaceted issue.

3. Stigmatization and Discrimination

Despite progress in destigmatizing mental health issues, addiction remains a stigmatized condition. Individuals struggling with addiction often face discrimination, hindering their access to employment, housing, and healthcare. A societal shift towards compassion and understanding is essential to break down these barriers.

The Role of Prevention

1. Early Intervention

Preventing addiction begins with early intervention and education. By fostering awareness about the risks and consequences of addictive behaviors, individuals can make informed choices and seek support before the chains of addiction tighten.

2. Education Programs

In schools and communities, education programs play a pivotal role in shaping attitudes and behaviors towards substances. Informing the younger generation about the dangers of addiction equips them with the knowledge to make healthier choices, breaking the cycle before it begins.

3. Mental Health Support

Recognizing the interplay between mental health and addiction is crucial for prevention efforts. Providing accessible mental health support and resources can address underlying issues that may contribute to the development of addictive behaviors.

Beyond Sobriety: Embracing a Holistic Approach

1. Addressing Underlying Issues

True recovery extends beyond mere sobriety; it involves addressing the underlying issues that contribute to addiction. Trauma, mental health disorders, and environmental factors must be acknowledged and treated to create a solid foundation for lasting change.

2. Fostering Resilience

Building resilience is a cornerstone of overcoming addiction. Individuals in recovery must develop coping mechanisms, stress management skills, and a support system that bolsters their ability to navigate life's challenges without resorting to addictive behaviors.

3. Redefining Success

In a society often fixated on conventional markers of success, redefining what success means for individuals in recovery is paramount. Celebrating milestones, both big and small, fosters a sense of accomplishment and reinforces the journey towards a fulfilling, addiction-free life.

Conclusion

Breaking the chains of addiction is an arduous yet transformative journey, encompassing physical, emotional, and societal dimensions. As we reflect on the dark side of human nature, understanding addiction is not only about acknowledging its existence but also about collectively dismantling the stigma that shrouds it. By fostering empathy, providing support, and embracing a holistic approach, we pave the way for individuals to emerge from the shadows, empowered and resilient, on their path to recovery.

Introduction

In the intricate tapestry of human relationships, there exists a dark thread that weaves its way through the subtle nuances of interaction - manipulation. This subtle art, often concealed beneath the surface of seemingly genuine connections, can have profound consequences on individuals and the dynamics of their relationships. In this exploration of the dark side of human nature, we delve into the tactics employed by manipulators and the far-reaching consequences of their actions.

The Anatomy of Manipulation

Understanding manipulation requires a dissection of its various facets. Manipulators employ a range of tactics to control, influence, and exploit others, often without their knowledge.

1. Gaslighting: Twisting Reality

One of the most insidious forms of manipulation is gaslighting, where the manipulator distorts the victim's perception of reality. This can involve subtle lies, denial of facts, or the creation of doubt, leaving the victim questioning their own sanity. Gaslighting erodes trust and fosters a sense of dependency on the manipulator.

2. Emotional Blackmail: Tugging at Heartstrings

Manipulators often use emotional blackmail to coerce others into compliance. This involves exploiting the emotions of the victim, employing guilt, fear, or pity to elicit the desired response. Emotional blackmail creates a power dynamic where the victim feels emotionally indebted to the manipulator, fostering a toxic cycle of dependency.

3. Selective Disclosure: Crafting a Facade

Manipulators are adept at revealing only selective information to create a specific image or narrative. By strategically disclosing certain details while withholding others, they shape perceptions and control the flow of information. This selective disclosure manipulates how others perceive the manipulator and the situation at hand.

The Consequences of Manipulative Behavior

The repercussions of manipulation extend beyond the immediate act, leaving a lasting impact on both individuals and their relationships.

1. Erosion of Trust: The Fragile Foundation

Trust is the cornerstone of any healthy relationship. Manipulation, however, corrodes this foundation, creating cracks that deepen over time. As the manipulator's deceit becomes apparent, trust shatters, leaving the victim grappling with the aftermath of betrayal.

2. Deterioration of Self-Esteem: The Silent Struggle

Victims of manipulation often experience a gradual erosion of self-esteem. Constant gaslighting, emotional blackmail, and other manipulative tactics chip away at the individual's confidence and self-worth. This internal struggle can lead to feelings of inadequacy, self-doubt, and a diminished sense of identity.

3. Isolation: Breaking Bonds

Manipulators thrive on isolating their victims, severing their connections with friends and family. By creating an environment of dependency, manipulators ensure their victims have no external support system. The resulting isolation intensifies the impact of the manipulation, making it even more challenging for the victim to break free.

Recognizing Manipulative Behavior

Awareness is the first step towards protecting oneself from manipulation. By recognizing the signs and understanding the tactics employed by manipulators, individuals can empower themselves to navigate relationships more effectively.

1. Trust Your Instincts: Intuition as a Guide

Intuition is a powerful tool in identifying manipulative behavior. If something feels off or if there's a persistent sense of unease, it's crucial to trust those instincts. Often, the subconscious mind picks up on subtle cues that the conscious mind may overlook.

2. Patterns of Behavior: Red Flags Unveiled

Manipulation is seldom a one-time occurrence. Recognizing patterns of behavior is essential in identifying manipulative tactics. Paying attention to consistent themes, such as deceit, guilt-tripping, or isolation, can reveal the true nature of a relationship.

Fostering open communication is a key defense against manipulation. Establishing a safe space for honest dialogue encourages transparency and discourages manipulative behavior. Creating an environment where individuals feel comfortable expressing their thoughts and concerns helps to dismantle the manipulator's power.

Conclusion

In the shadows of human relationships, the strings of manipulation are woven with precision and cunning. As we reflect on the dark side of human nature, it is imperative to shine a light on these subtle tactics that threaten the very fabric of our connections. By understanding the anatomy of manipulation, acknowledging its consequences, and actively recognizing manipulative behavior, we empower ourselves to navigate relationships with resilience and authenticity. In the end, it is through this awareness that we can hope to break free from the strings that bind us, fostering healthier, more genuine connections.

Introduction

Betrayal is a haunting echo that reverberates through the corridors of our lives, leaving indelible marks on our psyche. In the realm of human nature, the dark side often emerges in the form of betrayal, fracturing trust and shattering the foundations of relationships. This article delves into the intricate web of emotions, the psychological aftermath, and the arduous journey of rebuilding trust after a breach.

Understanding Betrayal

Betrayal, at its core, is the violation of trust. It can manifest in various forms, from infidelity in romantic relationships to disloyalty among friends or colleagues. The ripple effects of betrayal extend far beyond the initial breach, creating a complex tapestry of emotions that demand careful examination.

The Emotional Turmoil

The aftermath of betrayal is a tempest of emotions, ranging from anger and disbelief to profound sadness and vulnerability. The betrayed individual experiences a profound sense of loss, not only of the relationship itself but also of the trust that once bound them to the betrayer. Understanding and navigating this emotional turmoil is crucial for healing to commence.

Psychological Impact

Betrayal inflicts wounds on the psyche that may take considerable time to heal. Trust, once shattered, leaves behind scars that influence future relationships and interactions. Individuals may develop a heightened sense of skepticism, making it challenging to extend trust to others. The psychological impact extends beyond the individual, affecting their worldview and interpersonal dynamics.

The Role of Guilt and Shame

For the betrayer, guilt and shame become formidable adversaries. The realization of the pain inflicted upon someone close can lead to a profound internal struggle. Managing these emotions is crucial for personal growth and, ultimately, for contributing to the process of rebuilding trust. It requires introspection, accountability, and a genuine commitment to change.

The Dynamics of Rebuilding Trust

Rebuilding trust is akin to reconstructing a delicate structure from its shattered pieces. It demands patience, effort, and a mutual willingness to engage in the process. Both parties must be committed to understanding the root causes of betrayal and actively participating in the restoration of trust.

Communication as a Cornerstone

Open and honest communication serves as the cornerstone of trust rebuilding. Both the betrayed and the betrayer must express their feelings, fears, and expectations without reservation. A sincere dialogue fosters understanding, enabling the acknowledgment of mistakes and the formulation of a path forward.

Rebuilding Self-Trust

In the aftermath of betrayal, individuals often grapple with a diminished sense of self-worth and trust in their own judgment. Rebuilding self-trust is a vital component of the healing process. This involves introspection, self-forgiveness, and a commitment to personal growth. Seeking support from trusted friends, family, or mental health professionals can aid in this journey.

Cultivating Empathy

Empathy plays a pivotal role in the reconstruction of trust. Both parties must strive to understand each other's perspectives, acknowledging the pain and vulnerability on both sides. Cultivating empathy fosters a compassionate environment where healing can take root.

Setting Boundaries

Rebuilding trust necessitates the establishment of clear boundaries. These boundaries serve as safeguards against future breaches and provide a framework for rebuilding the relationship. Establishing and respecting each other's boundaries creates a sense of safety and predictability, fostering an environment conducive to trust restoration.

Forgiveness as a Healing Balm

Forgiveness is a potent healing balm in the aftermath of betrayal. It does not condone the betrayal but liberates the betrayed from the shackles of resentment. Forgiveness is a process, not a one-time event, and it requires a conscious decision to let go of the past and embrace the possibility of a renewed connection.

The Long Road to Rebuilding

Rebuilding trust is a gradual process that unfolds over time. It involves setbacks, moments of doubt, and a persistent commitment to the journey. Both individuals must be willing to invest the time and effort required, understanding that the road to rebuilding trust is a marathon, not a sprint.

Conclusion

Betrayal's echo is a haunting melody that lingers in the recesses of our consciousness, shaping our relationships and self-perception. Yet, amidst the wreckage, there exists the potential for renewal and growth. Rebuilding trust after a breach is a testament to the resilience of the human spirit, a journey that requires introspection, communication, empathy, and forgiveness. In navigating the aftermath of betrayal, individuals can emerge stronger, forging connections that transcend the shadows of the past.

Chapter 22. Reflections on the Shadows Within

Introduction

As we arrive at the concluding chapter of "Reflections on the Dark Side of Human Nature", it is essential to take a moment and reflect on the intricate journey we have embarked upon. The prologue to our exploration, aptly titled "Prologue to Shadows", set the stage for an introspective journey into the complexities of human nature. The chapters that followed delved deep into the shadows that linger within us, shedding light on the darker corners of our existence. In this concluding chapter, we will summarize key themes, explore potential solutions, and encourage reflection on the complex interplay of negative human attributes.

Acknowledging the Duality

Our journey began by acknowledging the duality of human existence - the coexistence of light and darkness within individuals and society. It was an invitation to confront and embrace the shadows that often elude our conscious awareness. Recognizing this dual nature sets the foundation for understanding rather than judging, a theme that runs through each exploration in this book.

Exploring the Roots of Violence

In Chapter 2, we delved into the roots of violence, unraveling the origins and psychological factors behind aggressive behavior. Understanding the deep-seated causes of violence is the first step towards addressing and mitigating its impact on individuals and societies. This exploration urges us to consider preventive measures and psychological interventions to break the cycle of violence.

Beyond Cruelty: Environmental Exploitation

Chapter 3 examined the environmental consequences of human actions, emphasizing the interconnectedness between our behavior and the health of our planet. A call to environmental stewardship, this chapter encourages a reevaluation of our relationship with nature and a commitment to sustainable practices to mitigate the adverse effects of environmental exploitation.

Silent Victims: The Dark Side of Animal Testing

The ethical concerns surrounding animal testing took center stage in Chapter 4. By scrutinizing the treatment of animals in research, we were prompted to reflect on our responsibility towards other living beings. This exploration encourages us to advocate for alternatives and humane practices in scientific research, fostering a more compassionate relationship with the animal kingdom.

Coercion and Consent: Unraveling the Complexities of Sexual Violence

Chapter 5 forced us to confront the painful reality of sexual violence and its far-reaching consequences. By analyzing the dynamics and impact of non-consensual acts, this chapter prompts us to reevaluate societal norms, promote consent education, and actively work towards creating a culture that condemns and prevents sexual violence.

Corruption: Unmasking the Misuse of Power

Chapter 6 delved into the pervasive issue of corruption at different levels of society. Understanding the consequences of corruption prompts us to advocate for transparency, accountability, and ethical leadership. It is a call to action for individuals and communities to resist and expose corruption, fostering a culture of integrity.

The Art of Deception: Unpacking the Layers of Dishonesty

Chapter 7 explored the intricate layers of dishonesty, unraveling the psychological mechanisms behind lying and manipulation. By understanding the roots of deceit, we can cultivate a culture of honesty and integrity, promoting genuine connections and dismantling the corrosive impact of deception on personal and societal levels.

Fortune at a Cost: The High Price of Greed

Our exploration of the societal consequences of greed in Chapter 8 revealed the destructive impact of unchecked avarice and self-centeredness. This chapter encourages a shift towards more equitable and sustainable economic systems, challenging us to question our values and redefine success beyond material wealth.

The Ugly Face of Bias: Discrimination Across Societal Lines

Chapter 9 addressed the various forms of prejudice and discrimination that permeate society. By recognizing the harmful impact of bias, we are prompted to promote diversity, equity, and inclusion. This exploration challenges us to confront our own biases and work towards dismantling systemic discrimination.

From Confidence to Arrogance: The Perils of Overestimating Self-Worth

Chapter 10 examined the destructive effects of excessive pride and entitlement. By acknowledging the thin line between healthy self-esteem and destructive egocentrism, we are prompted to cultivate humility and empathy. This exploration encourages a balance between individuality and interconnectedness.

The Ego Trap: Balancing Individuality with Empathy

Chapter 11 further explored the delicate balance between individuality and empathy. Recognizing the perils of egocentrism, this chapter calls for a harmonious integration of self-expression with a genuine understanding and concern for others. It is an invitation to foster a compassionate and interconnected world.

Green-Eyed Monsters: Jealousy and Envy in Everyday Life

Chapter 12 delved into the psychological impact and social consequences of envy. By understanding the roots of jealousy, we can cultivate empathy, resilience, and gratitude. This exploration encourages us to celebrate the success of others and recognize the toxicity of comparison.

The Intolerance Paradox: Navigating Diversity in a Globalized World

Chapter 13 addressed the challenges of fostering tolerance in an interconnected world. This exploration encourages us to embrace diversity and engage in open dialogues to overcome the paradox of intolerance. It is a call to break down cultural barriers and build bridges of understanding.

Stealing Trust: The Impact of Theft on Individuals and Society

Chapter 14 examined the emotional and societal repercussions of theft. By understanding the profound impact of stolen trust, we are prompted to advocate for justice and rehabilitation. This exploration encourages us to address the root causes of theft and work towards creating a society that supports rehabilitation over punitive measures.

White-Collar Crimes: Unraveling the Web of Financial Deceit

In Chapter 15, we investigated the world of white-collar crime and its far-reaching ramifications. This exploration prompts us to demand accountability, transparency, and ethical business practices. It is a call for systemic change to prevent financial deceit and protect individuals and communities.

Apathy in Action: The Consequences of Indifference

Chapter 16 discussed the societal implications of widespread apathy and disinterest. By recognizing the destructive consequences of indifference, we are prompted to cultivate empathy and actively engage in social issues. This exploration encourages us to break the cycle of apathy and contribute to positive social change.

Cyber Shadows: Crimes in the Digital Age

Chapter 17 analyzed the prevalence and impact of online crimes in the digital age. Understanding the nuances of cyber shadows prompts us to advocate for digital literacy, cybersecurity, and ethical online behavior. It is a call for collective responsibility to create a safer and more secure digital space.

Beyond Catcalling: The Harsh Reality of Street Harassment

Chapter 18 brought attention to the pervasive issue of street harassment faced by women in public spaces. By understanding the harsh reality of catcalling, we are prompted to challenge cultural norms, promote gender equality, and create safer public environments. This exploration encourages us to actively participate in the fight against street harassment.

Breaking the Chains: Understanding and Overcoming Addiction

Chapter 19 explored the complexities of addiction and its societal impact. By understanding the root causes of addiction, we are prompted to advocate for prevention, treatment, and destigmatization. This exploration encourages us to approach addiction with empathy and support those on the journey to recovery.

Strings Attached: The Art of Manipulation in Human Relationships

Chapter 20 delved into the tactics and consequences of manipulative behavior. Recognizing the subtle art of manipulation prompts us to cultivate healthy relationships built on trust and communication. This exploration encourages us to be vigilant against manipulation and promote genuine connections.

Betrayal's Echo: Rebuilding Trust After a Breach

Chapter 21 explored the psychological and relational aftermath of betrayal. By understanding the complexities of rebuilding trust, we are prompted to engage in open communication and forgiveness. This exploration encourages us to navigate the challenges of betrayal with resilience and empathy.

Reflections on the Shadows Within

As we reach the concluding chapter, it is crucial to reflect on the overarching themes that have emerged throughout our journey. We have encountered the shadows within us - violence, cruelty, deception, greed, bias, arrogance, jealousy, intolerance, theft, apathy, cybercrime, harassment, addiction, manipulation, and betrayal. Each exploration has invited us to confront these shadows, understand their origins, and consider potential solutions.

Potential Solutions

While the shadows within us may seem daunting, there is hope in recognizing that understanding is the first step towards transformation. To address the complexities of negative human attributes, we must collectively strive for the following solutions.

Education: Promote awareness and education to foster a deeper understanding of the roots and consequences of negative human behaviors.

Advocacy: Advocate for systemic changes that address the societal structures and norms contributing to the manifestation of dark human attributes.

Empathy: Cultivate empathy to bridge the gaps between individuals and communities, fostering a more compassionate and interconnected world.

Accountability: Demand accountability at personal, societal, and institutional levels to discourage and prevent negative behaviors.

Rehabilitation: Prioritize rehabilitation over punitive measures, recognizing the potential for personal growth and societal healing.

Cultural Change: Challenge cultural norms that perpetuate harmful behaviors and promote values of inclusivity, respect, and cooperation.

Personal Responsibility: Encourage individuals to reflect on their own actions, motivations, and biases, taking responsibility for personal growth and positive change.

Encouraging Reflection

As we conclude this journey, it is essential to encourage reflection on the complex interplay of negative human attributes. Each reader is invited to contemplate their own shadows, acknowledging the potential for growth, transformation, and collective change. By fostering a culture of introspection and self-awareness, we can contribute to a world that recognizes the shadows within, confronts them with courage, and strives for a brighter, more compassionate future.

In the end, "Reflections on the Dark Side of Human Nature" is not just a book; it is a mirror that invites us to gaze into the depths of our own humanity. It is a call to action, urging us to confront the shadows within and, in doing so, contribute to the ongoing narrative of human evolution.

"Reflections on the Dark Side of Human Nature" invites readers on a profound exploration of the intricacies inherent in the human psyche. In the introductory chapter, "Prologue to Shadows", the stage is set for a contemplative journey into the dualities of human existence. Acknowledging the coexistence of light and darkness within individuals and society, the book aims to understand, rather than judge, the nuanced aspects of negative human attributes. The subsequent chapters delve into diverse realms of human behavior, such as the roots of violence, environmental exploitation, animal testing, sexual violence, corruption, dishonesty, greed, bias, arrogance, jealousy, and many more.

Each chapter offers a deep analysis, unraveling the complexities and consequences of these shadows that shape our lives. The concluding chapter, "Reflections on the Shadows Within", summarizes key themes, explores potential solutions, and encourages readers to reflect on the intricate interplay of negative human attributes. This book serves as a thought-provoking guide, urging readers to contemplate the shadows that linger within and the profound impact they have on the individual and collective human experience.

ABOUT THE AUTHOR

Mr. C. P. Kumar is a retired Scientist 'G' from National Institute of Hydrology, Roorkee, Uttarakhand, India. He is also a Reiki Healer and Chakra Balancing practitioner (with pendulum dowsing) and offers Emotional Freedom Technique (EFT) to help individuals with emotional issues. Mr. Kumar has authored many books on technical, spiritual, and social topics.

For further details, you may visit his webpage
https://www.angelfire.com/nh/cpkumar/virgo.html